THE LAST TRAIN OUT

WELLESLEY MUIR

AMAZING FACTS

Roseville, CA

Printed in the USA

Published by
Amazing Facts, Inc.
PO Box 1058
Roseville, CA 95678-8058
800-538-7275

All royalties will be donated for mission work in the Upper Amazon Jungle of Peru.

Cover Design by Haley Trimmer

Text Design by Greg Solie — Altamont Graphics

Library of Congress Cataloging-in-Publication Data

Muir, Wellesley, 1926-
  Last train out / by Wellesley Muir.
     p. cm.
  ISBN 1-58019-199-1 (alk. paper)
  1. Neuendorff, Siegfried, 1933- 2. Missionaries--Peru--Biography. 3. Seventh-Day Adventists--Peru--Biography. 4. Missionaries--United States--Biography. 5. Seventh-Day Adventists--United States--Biography.
I. Title.

  BV2853.P7N486 2005
  286.7092--dc22

                              2005030944

06 07 08 09 10 • 5 4 3 2 1

Table of Contents

Acknowledgments

Siegfried Neuendorff, for sharing how God led his life.

Evelyn, my wife, for correcting my errors
and making helpful suggestions.

Dorothy Christman, for highlighting the most
important events in Siegfried's life.

God, for **His** promise: "I *will be* with you; ... When
you walk through the fire, you shall not be burned,
nor shall the flame scorch you" (Isaiah 43:2).

"We must live a twofold life—a life of thought and action, of
silent prayer and earnest work" (*Ministry of Healing*, 512).

Dedication

To **Don and Dorothy Christman**. While serving as president of
the Inca Union Mission, Pastor Christman encouraged Siegfried
Neuendorff in his ministry to reach jungle tribes with the gospel.

And to student missionaries who served with Siegfried
Neuendorff at the Unini Mission Station:

Barry Black

Dick Eberlein

Steven Farley

Bob Fetrick

Paul Mayberry

Allan Payne

"The greatest want of the world is the want of men—men who will
not be bought or sold, men who in their inmost souls are true and
honest, men who do not fear to call sin by its right name, men whose
conscience is as true to duty as the needle to the pole, men who
will stand for the right though the heavens fall" (*Education*, 57).

Chapter 1
Berlin in Flames

~

The old train's coal-burning steam engine belched heavy black smoke into the clear air on a bright spring morning. Ten-year-old Siegfried Neuendorff gazed out through the coach's dirty glass window. Thirty-five other boys his age, but all strangers, were also on board, ready to leave bomb-battered Berlin for a Hitler Youth Camp in German-occupied Poland.

Siegfried watched a woman approach. *It's Mutti, my mother. She found me. I wish I could jump out and hug her one more time.*

The whistle blew, and the train jerked forward. Siegfried saw tears trickle down Mutti's cheeks as she threw him a kiss. He waved, keeping his eyes glued on her, as the train moved away from Berlin's downtown railway station. The engine picked up speed, and his mother vanished.

Huge signs painted on walls along the tracks said, "Psst Feind Hört Mit!" ["The enemy is listening!"] The German Reich constantly warned citizens to be quiet and not give clues to American or Russian spies regarding troop movements.

The train moved past bombed-out buildings. Flames still leaped through the ruins of a large industrial plant struck the night before by allied bombs. *Why all the destruction?* It was impossible for a young boy to understand.

Listening to the monotonous "clickity-clack" of wheels hugging steel rails, Siegfried leaned back in the hard seat. Sad, lonely, he felt warm tears form in his eyes. *Why is Hitler taking me away from my parents? Will I ever see Mutti and Papa again?*

The train chugged through the German countryside leaving the burning city of Berlin behind. Fearful for the future, the heartsick boy remembered how his mother taught him to pray. Leaning forward in his seat, he closed his eyes. "Dear Jesus, please keep bombs from falling on Papa and Mutti and keep me safe." During the long, jolting train ride to Poland, Siegfried recalled what his parents told him about his early years.

⌒

After listening to wedding bells ring, Walter and Lina Neuendorff moved into a small wood-frame house built in a Berlin suburb by the young husband. Electricity brought light to their home, but Lina carried all their water from a public well. A little over a year later, Johannes, their first son was born.

Walter, a skilled cabinetmaker, rode to work on a bicycle where he fashioned fine furniture for Knoblauch. Known for quality, people traveled for miles to purchase the custom cabinets he built. When Lina wasn't cleaning, cooking, mending, or carrying water, she went out on the city streets and sold Christian books. She wanted all to know about the Christ she dearly loved.

On January 30, 1933, Hitler became chancellor of Germany, quickly turning the country into a Nazi dictatorship. The Neuendorffs worried, *What will happen to our country now?* Hitler's book, *Mein Kampf,* made his intentions clear. "Germans are a super race. We will conquer the world."

On November 23, 1933, the same year Hitler came to power, Lina awoke with intense labor pains. Walter had left for his shop, so after dressing, she slipped into a heavy winter coat. Snowflakes fell as she rushed across the street to Grandma Bohlmann's house and pounded on the door.

"Please come! I need you now!" Lina spoke urgently as the door opened. Hurrying to the Neuendorff home, Grandma helped Lina get comfortable. Soon a baby began to cry. "You've got another boy!" Grandma shouted as she handed Lina her new son. That night Walter and Lina huddled near their old wood stove as Lina nursed the baby. Reaching for her husband's hand, she asked, "What are we going to name our newest son?"

"I haven't really thought much about it," Walter replied. "I was hoping for a girl."

"I have a suggestion then," Lina squeezed her husband's hand. "Why don't we call him Siegfried? It's an old German name that means 'victory and peace.' I want this boy to find victory and live a life of peace. You know about the Siegfried line between Germany and France."

A year later, although the birth of a daughter, Krista, brought joy to the Neuendorffs, Germans were finding it increasingly difficult to keep food on the table. Few families had money to order custom furniture. The Great Depression in the United States had finally spread to Europe, and German families suffered.

With a shortage of wood, it became difficult to keep the house warm. Tiny Krista, only six-months-old, contracted pneumonia. Lina did all she could to save her daughter, yet the child only got worse. She prayed, "Please Lord, You gave us Krista. Please, if it's Your will, help her get well."

When Krista died, Walter built a tiny coffin and the family placed the baby in the cold ground to wait for an answer to a mother's prayer at the resurrection. Siegfried and Johannes were too young to understand.

The boys called their mother Mutti, and she often read Bible stories telling her sons about Jesus. She wanted her sons to experience love and grace. She wanted them to obey. She taught them to pray. Still grieving the loss of her daughter, Mutti claimed a Bible promise—"All things work together for good to those who love God" (Roman 8:28).

With no money to buy an automobile, Papa used his bicycle for family transportation. He often peddled Johannes around on the handlebar. As Siegfried grew, Papa decided to take him too. A neighbor saw Walter pedaling down the street with a curly headed blue-eyed blond youngster on the handlebars. "Hey, Neuendorff," he called out. "You really have a cute little girl!"

"A girl?" Papa growled. "This is my son, Siegfried!"

Reaching home, Papa lifted his boy off the handlebars. "You little dummy," he said. "Why do you have to look like a girl?" Troubled by a neighbor's comments, Walter began leaving Siegfried home, taking Johannes instead.

Siegfried wondered, *Why does Papa always favor Johannes?* Insecurity began to grow in his young heart.

When Johannes and Siegfried were old enough to attend kindergarten, their mother got a job working for an insurance company to help meet household expenses. The parents believed the Bible admonition, "If anyone will not work, neither shall he eat" (2 Thessalonians 3:10).

The boys were given after-school chores: water and wood to carry, weeds to pull, and in season, fruit and berries to pick. Inside, there were dishes to wash, floors to clean, furniture to dust, and—Siegfried's favorite job—stacking bricks. However, where Johannes pleased his father in all his chores, Siegfried was often scolded. "You dumb bunny! Can't you do better than that?"

One afternoon in September 1939, six-year-old Siegfried played in the yard. *What's the strange noise I hear?* It sounded like dozens of cows all mooing at the same time. He ran to his mother. "Mutti, when did our neighbors get cows?"

"Siegfried," she replied, "Our neighbors don't have cows. Germany's at war! It's not the sound of cows. The siren you hear is an air raid warning! Enemy bombers are on their way to attack. Our city doesn't have bomb shelters yet. There's no place to hide. Let's pray and ask Jesus to protect us."

Fearful for the future, Berliners built bomb shelters in every district. Some were two stories underground. Others mushroomed three stories above ground. All bunkers were built with steel reinforced concrete walls two- to three-feet thick, making them reasonably safe. During bombing raids, women and children ran to the public bunkers. This proved difficult at night because the Reich ordered total blackouts during raids. Any visible light was considered a major crime punishable by imprisonment or a heavy fine. Like other men in the neighborhood, Herr Neuendorff dug a simple bomb shelter in the back yard. Men usually stayed near their homes to protect their property and put out fires ignited by incendiary bombs.

The Neuendorff family, assigned to bunker cabin number 33, shared with families who had no bunker space. Papa cautioned his family, "When you hear the air-raid siren, run to the shelter immediately. A minute's delay may cost your life."

Frequent raids filled the hearts of parents and children with fear. Racing to bomb shelters became a nightly routine. Neighborhood women whose husbands were on the battlefront and widows who lost their husbands in the war often came to Siegfried's mother. "Frau Neuendorff, please pray for us." After praying, she shared Bible verses that gave her family and neighbors hope. "You shall not be afraid of the terror by night. ... He shall give His angels charge over you" (Psalm 91:5, 11).

Many times after an attack, Papa took his family out to witness the destruction. Siegfried saw entire city blocks of homes in flames. One night, stables near the Neuendorff home were hit by incendiary bombs. The young boy witnessed a horrifying scene. "Papa," Siegfried screamed, "Look at the horses running around like torches." A backyard shelter a few houses down the street from the Neuendorff's received a direct hit. Only the charred flesh of a German shepherd dog was found. The residents totally vaporized during the blast.

Schoolboys played with shrapnel and unexploded bombs until one day a boy's hand was blown off. The Reich warned citizens to avoid handling toys or anything attractive that might contain explosives. Siegfried found a suspicious looking carpenter's pencil and informed police. They came and defused it.

A Daimler-Benz factory manufacturing tanks near the Neuendorff residence seemed to be a favorite target. Planes dropped flares attached to parachutes lighting up Berlin. A second group of planes swooped in dropping bombs, filling the air with deafening sounds of explosions.

Everything came to a stop when air-raid sirens blared. People fled to the nearest shelter. Siegfried froze with fear each time he heard the steady hum of B-17 bombers. One evening Papa hid in the backyard shelter while his family rushed to the public bunker. A shrill whistling sound ended in a sudden thud. *What's that?* he wondered.

Morning light revealed the end of an incendiary bomb sticking out of the ground in Neuendorff's back yard. It had penetrated two feet of solid soil, four layers of large clinker blocks and a four-inch header. Mutti looked at her husband. "God worked a miracle for you. Three more inches and the bomb would have pierced your skull. You were sitting right under it. Praise God for keeping my sons from being fatherless," she said.

A hunchbacked elderly widow lived near the Neuendorff's. One evening a bomb struck her house setting it on fire. Everyone ran with buckets of water to put out the blaze. In spite of earnest efforts to douse the fire, the woman's home burned to the ground.

Returning to their home, Papa saw a light through the keyhole of their tool shed. Investigating, he found a bomb surrounded by wood shavings smoldering on the dirt floor. While flooding it with water, he thought, *This is amazing. Our tool shed should be in flames!*

One night the family returned from the shelters and found a hole in the wall of their house. Shrapnel had penetrated three separate walls and landed next to a box by the stove. After another bombing, Mutti opened the pantry door and found an entire cabinet filled with canned fruit and jams lying on a cement floor—not one jar broken. In a few weeks the entire economy came to a halt. With little food available, the family enjoyed not just "bread and water," but also fruit and jam.

As the war initiated by the Nazis accelerated, Hitler found it increasingly difficult to fulfill his pledge to allow no one to suffer hunger or cold. Ration stamps for bread, butter, flour, sugar, and potatoes were distributed to everyone except prisoners, foreigners, and Jews. People were forbidden to go directly to farmers. Police confiscated all food obtained directly from the source.

With their own garden and several fruit trees, the Neuendorffs kept food on the table, but it wasn't going that well for most. Tante [Auntie] Friedel, Mutti's Jewish friend, got food because she was married to a German. When her prosperous Jewish relatives began to suffer for lack of food, she asked Mutti for help.

Tante collected clothing, jewelry, and china from wealthy relatives giving them to Mutti as fair payment for food. Each week, Mutti traveled to her birthplace, a country village 40 miles south of Berlin. She traded the items received from Tante to relatives and friends for food and carried it back to Berlin.

Mutti knew it was prohibited to carry food. She reasoned, *It's also true that we are to "obey God rather than man." Jesus said,*

"I was hungry and you gave Me food." Then He added, *"Inasmuch as you did it to one of the least of these My brethren, you did it to Me"* (Matthew 25:35, 40).

Before each trip she prayed, "Lord, please protect me and help me get the food you impress friends to share so I can distribute it to starving Jews." Not even once did police stop her or challenge her. On one trip, she carried three sacks of potatoes. A policeman confiscated all the potatoes from folks sitting in front. Then he stepped over her three sacks and took all the potatoes from the people sitting behind her. "I know God was with me," she told her family.

An adult caught giving food to a Jew in Nazi Germany could be sent before a firing squad. "Siegfried," she called, "I need your help. This is a dangerous mission, but God will be with you. I want you to take food to hungry Jewish families. You will knock once, pause and knock three more times in quick succession. They will know it's you and come to the door."

"If this is what God wants me to do, I will do my best," Siegfried replied.

Each Sunday Siegfried took a streetcar to the center of town with his cargo of food products. He'd climb many stairs in apartment buildings, stand in front of the large doors, and knock. The door would open slightly. A feminine voice would whisper, "Siegfried, is that you? Are you alone?"

"Yes, I'm alone."

The big door would open quietly and Siegfried slipped in quickly. Only when they were sure it was safe, the husband would come out of the closet and thank the young benefactor with a big handshake. After leaving the food, Siegfried slipped out quietly and went to the next apartment on his list. One man said, "You are a very brave boy to help us when you could be sent to a concentration camp or shot for your kindness."

Papa and Mutti took another risk. They sheltered a 13-year-old Jewish boy for several months. He could have stayed longer, but his mother missed him so much that she asked him to come home. He apparently died in a gas chamber.

Adolf Hitler, a professed Roman Catholic, neither publicly encouraged or attacked religion, but he hated Jews. Siegfried's father, influenced by rebel pastor Louis Conradi, became disenchanted with his religion, yet he supported his family in their faith. Each Sabbath, Mutti took her two sons on a streetcar to attend the Seventh-day Adventist Church. Frequently, power outages kept streetcars from running, but in rain, snow, or sunshine, the mother and her boys walked five miles to church and another five miles back to their home after the service was over.

In winter, baths were taken in the bedroom with just a small pan of hot water—summer, in the backyard.

Shoes were also difficult to obtain and Mutti shared her own worn walking shoes with Siegfried. She even changed the buttons so her winter overcoat would open from left to right and could be worn by her son.

When Siegfried turned 10, a new law enacted by the Nazis required youth 10-years-old and up to register as members of Hitler's Youth Organization. Unless Siegfried and Johannes signed up, the family would not continue receiving food stamps.

Chapter 2

The Russians Are Coming

P lanning for his future utopian society, Hitler decided to save Germany's most promising boys from the constant danger of air raids by shipping them out of the country. Johannes went to Czechoslovakia. Siegfried, assigned to Band 200, Group 15, was scheduled to go to Poland.

While walking her son to Berlin's railroad station, Mutti agonized, *This is the worst thing I've ever had to do. The government has my oldest son. Now they're taking my baby.* With Russians moving in from the east and Americans from the west, she realized that she might never see her children again. *All I can do is leave them in God's hands.*

At the station, she gave her boy one last hug. "Siegfried, if you don't do anything else, pray. God will protect you." With an aching heart, she watched her 10-year-old boy board the train and disappear. Running along the track, she spotted her son sitting next to a window and threw him one final kiss as the train moved out of the station.

During the long, boring journey, Siegfried listened to the relentless "clack, clack, clack" of metal wheels striking joints in the steel rails. Late in the afternoon, the train crossed the Warta River. Continuing to their destination in the heart of Poland, the train finally screeched to a stop.

As the new Hitler Youth stepped off the train, they were met by Frau Friederich, a chubby matron with curly blond hair. "I'm your house mother," she declared. She led the boys to an old classroom filled with bunk beds and mattresses stuffed with straw. Each boy was assigned to a bunk and issued two bars of soap: one, rough soap, to wash their clothes, and the other, finer soap, for bathing and washing their hands and face.

As property of the Reich, the boys were to be disciplined and trained to help Hitler in his conquest of the world. Classes began the next morning with a drillmaster teaching them to march and obey orders. They were told not to have contact with the Polish people in the area.

With food scarce, the boys were to eat all that was given them—nothing was to be wasted. After a long Sunday morning march, the boys fell in line in front of the mess hall. With plates in their hands, they marched in and were served potatoes, peas, and fish. Siegfried studied the fish closely. *It doesn't have scales! What did Mutti teach me about unclean foods?*

Siegfried had always depended on his mother to choose the right food for him. Now he had to make his own choice, knowing that any food he wasted could bring severe punishment. Yet he also remembered Mutti reading how "Daniel purposed in his heart that he would not defile himself with the portion of the king's meat" (Daniel 1:8 KJV).

Lonely and far from home, Siegfried thought, *I know Jesus doesn't want me to eat unclean food, but what am I going to do? I'm really hungry!* Still, determined to follow the Bible and not cause trouble for himself, he quietly offered the fish to his new friends. The boys were already busy cleaning fish bones. "We can't eat any more!"

Panicked, a new idea flashed in Siegfried's mind. *No one's watching. I'll put it in my pocket!* He moved his hand slowly across his plate, grabbed the fish, and shoved it in his pocket. With no fish to eat, he finished first and quickly excused himself.

After returning his plate to the kitchen, he rushed to the outhouse in back of the dormitory. *This is great. I'm the only one here.* He hurriedly dropped the fish down the hole. *No one will ever know.*

Late that afternoon, Siegfried was called to the director's office. He sat directly in front of the usually jolly Frau Friederich, her piercing blue eyes looking right through him. "Siegfried," she asked, "What have you done?"

"Me?" he asked, with as much innocence as he could muster. "Yes, you!" she barked. "I see you don't like Hitler's food. You need to be punished!"

How does she know? He wondered. *What will she do? Will she make me stand in a corner while the other boys poke fun at me? Will she beat me with a stick?* Terrified, he expected the very worst for purposing not to eat any unclean food.

"Well, Siegfried, you won't be eating again until you're ready to eat what's served."

It was worse than he imagined. *Will I ever eat again?* Taller than any of the other boys, he always felt hungry. He had even mended boys socks to get extra food. *I can hardly make it from one meal to the next now. I'll die before I get food again!*

For the next meal, Siegfried was ordered to stay in his room, seated on his bed, until all the other boys were finished eating. As the tempting smell of food wafted over him, he felt his faith being tested like never before. *I've never been this hungry! Where are the angels? Where are the ravens that brought food to Elijah?*

Suddenly the door to his dormitory opened slightly. "Siegfried, are you by yourself?" The whisper was barely audible.

"Yes, I'm alone." Quickly the classmate stepped inside and closed the door quietly. "I brought you a sandwich," he said. Siegfried took the food gratefully and began to scarf it down. A few moments later, another boy snuck in with another sandwich. Soon, more boys came with food. Siegfried kept eating, but he couldn't possibly eat everything that had been brought.

All his friends had broken the rule about taking food out of the mess hall, so they didn't dare go back with the leftovers. Once again, Siegfried decided that dumping the food into the outhouse was the best solution. *I hope this works this time!*

But in a little less that 24 hours, Siegfried got a message. "Frau Friederich wants to see you in her office. You must go immediately."

Siegfried's knees shook as he sat in front of a very serious-looking matron. *What will she do to me now?*

"This has to stop," she demanded. "You are a bad influence on the other boys. You've got them breaking the rules by bringing you food. This can't go on any longer."

Tears rolled down Siegfried's ruddy cheeks. *I can't go any longer without food.* He prayed silently and then braced himself. "Frau Friederich, I broke your rules. But I couldn't eat the fish. Please write to my mother and ask her to explain why I couldn't eat the fish."

Days later, Siegfried was summoned back to the matron's office. He expected more trouble, but a smile broke across her big round face. "Now I understand why you didn't eat the fish." She held up a letter from Mutti!

Dear Frau Friederich,

We are believers in God and follow dietary rules found in sacred Scripture. Please excuse our son from eating unclean meat or fish. Since he's not always sure what's clean or unclean, he prefers no meat at all. Thank you for understanding that he's not rebellious. He just wants to follow his conscience.

Lina Neuendorff

The matron put down the letter and said, "From now on, if we serve meat or fish, just bring it to me, and I will give you my dessert."

Wonderful! Siegfried felt jubilant. *God answered my prayer. I won't starve to death after all.* Siegfried smiled at the director. "Thank you. Please forgive me for the trouble I caused you." Walking back to his bunk, he wanted to shout. *My problem's solved.* He felt joy for standing up for what he believed to be right.

I can't believe she's going to give me her dessert!

⌒⌒⌒

The attitude of Papa and Mutti toward Hitler's evil war had rubbed off on their younger son long before he was sent to the youth camp. So when an instructor announced that a group of men just attempted to kill Hitler, Siegfried flashed a brief smile thinking that no one would see him.

The teacher suddenly shouted, "Hold on, boy! You can't do that. You're disrespecting our leader. Stand at attention," he barked. "March to the front of the room!"

Obeying immediately, Siegfried thought, *I've made a terrible mistake.*

"Why did you smile?" the teacher demanded.

Siegfried stood in silence. "You rebel," the teacher growled. "You can stand at attention for one hour."

Siegfried tried his best to stand still. Egged on by the instructor, the others boys poked fun at him. The hour seemed to pass by endlessly for the young man nearing his eleventh birthday.

Back in Germany, the Hitler propaganda machine kept churning, "The war will soon be won. Germany will be in charge of the world." Little by little, German families began to discover the real truth. The attempt to conquer Moscow had failed. At Stalingrad, an entire army had been vanquished. And the battle on the beaches of Normandy, D-Day, had proven utterly disastrous for the Nazis. Moreover, the Russians were already at the doorstep to the Hitler Youth Camp in Poland.

Mutti worried about her son. *I must get to Siegfried before it's too late. If he ends up in the hands of the Russians, I'll never see him again.* It was a daunting task, especially when the Reich forbade civilians from traveling more than 60 miles at a time.

But the desperate mother had a plan, using the clothing she'd bartered for when exchanging food with her Jewish friends. *I will use these to save my son.* She boarded a train to Poland, trading a garment for 60 miles of travel. Instead of getting off after the 60 miles, she offered clothing for another 60 miles. Over and over she repeated the dangerous routine, until finally she reached Poland.

After disembarking from the train, she went directly to Frau Friederich's office and without the mandatory, "Heil Hitler!" announced, "I've come to take my son."

"Never!" the matron insisted. "Your son belongs to the German government. He must stay here."

Worried, Mutti answered, "You've had my son for a year. Thank you for the care you've given him. He has loved the desserts you gave him." She turned and walked out of the office, determined to find her boy.

As she headed for the dormitory, she saw a group of boys just returning from their drills. She spotted Siegfried immediately. He had grown much taller since she saw him.

Shocked, Siegfried saw his mother. *Is this real? Are my eyes deceiving me?* Siegfried ran to his mother and fell into her arms. "Mutti! Mutti! How did you get here?"

"God helped me," Mutti exclaimed. "Now, Siegfried," she whispered. "Get your coat and anything else important to you. We're going to take a walk." Afterward, she grabbed his hand and led him out of the camp.

They walked to the home of a Polish farmer, and knowing that just about every German she would run into would be searching for food, she traded the rest of her fine clothing for food as a way of bartering for miles on her way back to Berlin. On the day they returned, the announcement came that Siegfried's train was the last train out. There would be no more.

Safely home with their youngest, Mutti told her husband, "God prompted me to act at the right time."

Terror reigned down every night, as regular and intense bombings started fires that often lasted for days. The Allies' front lines moved closer still. It had become so bad that Papa insisted Mutti and Siegfried travel 40 miles to the village Mutti was born. He said, "Heavy fighting is expected soon. You and Siegfried better take the train to Wiesenburg and stay with your sister. The police should allow you to make the trip."

Before leaving the next morning, Mutti hugged her husband fearing she might never see him again. "I'll be praying that angels will keep you safe." She waved goodbye to her Walter.

Late that day, mother and son moved in with Aunt Ida, Mutti's youngest sister. A few days later, a German soldier showed up asking for shelter. "The Russians are coming," he said. "If they find me in a military uniform, I'll be killed or sent to Siberia." Aunt Ida gave him civilian clothing and burned his uniform. Years later, Ida received a letter from the soldier's wife thanking her for saving her husband's life.

Siegfried joined his mother and aunt in praying that their village would be captured by Americans and not the Red Army. One day, they took their bikes and started riding to Magdeburg hoping to buy a little sugar. Soon they met a crowd of people on bicycles coming in the opposite direction. The riders shouted,

"The Russians are coming! Go back home! The Americans are stopped at Magdeburg."

They turned around and raced back toward their village. When they arrived, Siegfried helped Mutti and Aunt Ida hang a large white sheet on the front of the house as a sign of surrender, hoping it would be enough to keep soldiers from firing on them. Then they waited. Nothing happened for two long days. Then suddenly on the third day, two black cars, followed by trucks and tanks, roared out of the forest into their village. The invading Russians kept on driving, right through the village, and never fired a shot. However, occupation forces soon followed, combing every house for German soldiers. One Russian soldier spotted a Bible on the table and pointed to it. With the little German he knew, he made it clear that he too was a Christian and appreciated that book. A Russian officer standing outside saw what was going on and ordered the soldier to leave the house.

Occupation under the Russian forces was often very difficult. One Russian saw a guitar in the house and asked to borrow it. He never brought it back.

On another day, a Russian soldier came by the house and asked Mutti to step outside. Siegfried worried, *What will happen to my mother?* It proved worse than he could imagine.

The Russian began forcing his mom along. Realizing the soldier intended to rape her, Mutti started shouting, "Commandant! Commandant!" The soldier then tried to force her to the ground. Finally in total desperation, she prayed, "Lord, help me!" Instantly the strong soldier drew back from his attack and walked away.

It's a miracle, Mutti thought. *God put fear in this man's heart.* "Thank you, Lord," she prayed.

Siegfried's aunt and Mutti realized that it wasn't safe for the family to be alone. So they decided to move to their older sister's home. Without delay, they took Siegfried and walked across the village to his Aunt Else's larger house. The adults slept in large beds, and Siegfried and his cousins slept on the floor.

That evening a Russian officer, looking for a place to camp with his men, checked the house to see if it would be safe. Seeing the children on the floor, he pointed his sword at Siegfried and mumbled something in Russian. *Is he planning to kill me?* Frightened,

Siegfried could barely move. But in broken German, the officer explained to Mutti, "Your boy looks like my nephew. He makes me feel homesick."

He then ordered his men to set up camp in the house. Turning to the women, he said, "Call me if anyone knocks on the door." The officer and his men hunkered down for the night, singing melancholy songs in Russian until they fell asleep. Later that evening, after midnight, a soldier began pounding on the door. The women nervously called on the officer , who opened the door to a drunk soldier looking for trouble. The officer quickly dispatched the problem, and two days later left the family's house with his soldiers without doing any harm.

~

Back in Berlin, the neighborhood around the Neuendorff home had turned into a war zone. Artillery shells from two fighting forces flew over the house and more deadly fires broke out. *At least I'm not out there fighting,* Walter consoled himself. His employer claimed he was vital to the war effort, and he felt blessed to stay home and work building ammunition boxes and coffins.

Desperate, Hitler ordered everyone, from grandfathers to teenagers, to register as members of the Volkssturm, or the "People's Storm Troops." All radios were to be left at the draft headquarters. Papa knew it was because Hitler didn't want his people to hear the real news about the war.

He went to the registration center along with the few other men still left in the area. While there, he asked for permission to go to the bathroom, walked out a back door, and never returned. The situation in the neighborhood continued to deteriorate. A mother and daughter who attended Mutti's church asked to hide in the Neuendorff's attic for fear of being raped.

Walter also knew there could be a lot of looting. He opened all the doors and windows in the house, took down the curtains, rolled up the carpets, and left dirty dishes in the sink. The scheme appeared to work perfectly, as soldiers walked through the house, saw the mess, and left without taking anything.

On April 30, 1945, Hitler committed suicide in a Berlin bunker. The war ended a few days later when Russians occupied Berlin. Papa longed to unite with his family, but transportation of all kinds came to a halt for lack of parts. Not even bicycle tires were available. He left Berlin riding on the rims. Soon he was stopped, and the bicycle confiscated. So Walter continued his journey along deserted streets on foot.

Near the outskirts of the city, a Russian soldier called him to halt. "What's your name?" he demanded.

"I'm Walter Neuendorff."

"And you're a Nazi soldier!" the Russian declared.

"No, I'm not!"

"Yes, you are. You're going to Siberia!"

"You can't do that to me! I'm a civilian, and I've never been in the military." Without warning, the Russian soldier struck him in the head, knocking his hat off. *This occupation is worse than the bombings,* he thought, trying to regain his composure. "Sir, my wife's gone so I haven't had a haircut for quite a while. I'm on my way to see her now. Do you think a German soldier would have long hair like mine?"

Amazingly, the Russian answered, "You're right, Herr Neuendorff. Go see your wife." *Mutti must be praying for me ... Long hair saved me from being a prisoner of war. I could have been on the way to Siberia.*

Papa trudged on, even as his ill-fitting shoes started hurting his feet, and he developed blisters. After walking nearly 40 miles on lonely roads, he felt like giving up.

And then while entering the Wiesenburg forest, a Russian soldier on horse appeared back suddenly appeared and without speaking a word, stayed by his side until he left the forest and the lights of the village appeared. As quickly as they appeared, the horse and rider vanished.

My wife would say it's an angel. Yet even with the village so close, the tight shoes and the blisters were killing him. *I can't take another step.* No longer able to stand, Walter fell to his knees.

That evening, his family awoke to strange noises in the street. Lifting the curtains, they saw a man crawling toward the house on his hands and knees.

Aunt Else whispered, "Lina, it looks like Walter." Siegfried pushed the curtain higher for a better look. He shouted, "It's Papa!"

When Papa's feet healed, he took Mutti and Siegfried and got a ride in a horse and buggy on the road to Berlin. After a couple of miles, the driver informed them that he would go no farther. They were forced to walk the rest of the way. Struggling to keep up with his parents, Siegfried fell farther and farther behind. Normally energetic, He grew weak from the meager diet of the past few weeks. Entering Berlin, his legs finally locked up. "You slowpoke," his tired father complained. Walter picked up his son and carried him the rest of the way home.

Chapter 3
Goodbye Berlin

M ore than a million people died or fled Europe's largest industrial center as the Allied bombs destroyed nearly a third of Berlin. In the weeks following the war, the Soviets stripped the city of most of its functioning industrial equipment. Although gradually, looting and shooting subsided under the Russian occupation, the city lay in ruins.

Siegfried's brother, Johannes, who had been stationed as a Hitler Youth in Czechoslovakia, hadn't been heard from for months. The Hitler Youth organization disorganized as the war began winding down, leaving the boys to defend for the themselves.

Johannes found himself in Bavaria, located in southern Germany. While there, he and a friend watched from a second story window as Americans and Germans faced off in battle. When his friend was shot in the arm, they decided to separate and find safer places to stay. Johannes decided to try the countryside, begging for food and a place to sleep. One farmer he approached asked, "Do you know how to pray?" Only after Johannes said the Lord's Prayer did the kind farmer give him some bread.

Mutti asked church members at the Mariendorf Adventist Church to pray for her missing son. Several days later, she looked out the window and saw Johannes standing by the garden gate. A total stranger had picked him up in Bavaria and brought him more than 500 miles, dropping him off in front of the family's home in Berlin. Mutti wondered if the stranger had really been an angel. *Praise God, He has brought our family together!*

Even though Papa's attitude toward religion and the church soured further during the war and under Communist rule, Mutti was not left discouraged. Food became extremely scarce under the Soviets, yet the Lord supplied their needs. As other families were forced to eat weeds, Mutti harvested apples, pears, plums, currants, and gooseberries in their own yard. They also gleaned potatoes from the field of a farmer friend.

More fortunate than many, they also had firewood for cooking and heating. A cabinet shop where Papa worked let him take home wood scraps. At best, however, life during the first few years after World War II became nothing more than a struggle to survive.

Some six months after the Russian invasion, the Allies divided Berlin into four sectors. The Neuendorffs felt blessed to live the American zone. Later their city simply became East and West Berlin, and they watched in horror as the Russians dismantled industries in the east.

The Americans, however, built up West Berlin, allowing families to resume a more normal life. Papa dreamed that his sons would someday become accomplished musicians. When he offered the boys the opportunity to take piano lessons, Johannes jumped at the chance. But Siegfried resisted, annoyed that his Papa still seemed to favor his brother. "I'm not interested."

Papa frowned. "You'll never do anything worth while."

Still, the brash refusal to please his father tore at his conscience. After a few weeks, he pulled his mother aside. "I'll study piano if you promise not to tell Papa." She agreed, and Siegfried began practicing secretly. Soon he played well enough to work on a duet with Johannes. With Mutti's encouragement, they planned a special audition.

"Papa," Mutti called. "Come here for a minute." He entered the living room where his boys had been waiting for him and sat down. Siegfried and Johannes, both at the piano, began playing together. Tears began streaming down their Papa's face as he listened to their music.

A few days later, Siegfried woke up with a terrible headache. He felt so hot, like he was burning up. His mother felt his warm body, confirming he was seriously sick. She did her best to care for her boy, but he steadily grew worse each passing hour.

Questions began filling his mind. *What will happen to me if I die? I'm 13-years-old and I've never been baptized.* He'd heard his mother read the story of Nicodemus many times. He couldn't get the words of Jesus out of his mind. "Except a man be born of water and of the Spirit, he cannot enter into the kingdom of God" (John 3:5).

By evening, Siegfried, convinced he was dying, called Mutti. "Please pray for me," he pled. "If I get well, I want to study the Bible and be baptized." Mutti had been waiting for those words from her son for a long time. Since his birth, she'd asked God to bless Siegfried and prepare him for God's kingdom. It had been so difficult with his father's influence, but she could see the Holy Spirit working strongly now.

"Dear God," she prayed. "Please, if it's your will, help Siegfried get well. Teach him how to serve you and help others. Forgive his sins and give him a home in heaven. Amen" Afterward, Mutti brought a large glass of cool water and placed a kiss on his hot forehead. "Good night, son. I hope you feel better tomorrow."

Siegfried tossed and turned in his bed. *I do want to be saved.* He also knew his mother wanted him to get well and serve God. He fell asleep wondering what serving God might involve.

The next morning came fast. Without thinking, he leaped out of bed with energy. His fever was gone! *This is wonderful.* Siegfried dressed quickly and marched into the kitchen where his mother was preparing breakfast. He hadn't eaten for 36 hours because of his sickness, but now he couldn't wait to fill his empty stomach. "Mutti," he said, "God answered your prayer. I feel wonderful." While eating a delicious breakfast, he said, "I must keep my promise to God. I want Pastor Franz Dombrowsky to give me Bible studies."

When his studies began, the pastor emphasized the need for a right relationship with God. "Jesus is the only way to heaven. We cannot save ourselves. The Savior died on the cross to pay for our sins. His gift of grace inspires love that leads us to obey His commandments. 'This is love, that we walk according to His commandments'" (2 John 6).

Then on October 11, 1947, Siegfried, along with his brother Johannes and other youth, was baptized. Coming up out of the water, Siegfried felt determined to be faithful to his baptismal vows for the rest of his life. This decision would be tested many times.

In one day during the war, Siegfried and his dad watched 2,000 bombers fly over their home. After more than 147 bombing raids, Berlin's buildings stood like lifeless skeletons. Such devastation had a terrible impact on the education of children all through Germany, and that included the Neuendorff boys.

Siegfried should have completed eight grades, but only finished three. One teacher, however, saw much potential in them. "Your boys have bright minds," he told the parents. "They should attend Eckner-Oberreal School." Siegfried knew it was an incredible privilege to go to such an elite school. But soon, he realized he'd never really learned how to study. After three years, his grades were bad enough that the principal was about to expel him. He approached his parents and begged, "Please let me go to a trade school where I can learn to use my hands."

Mutti arranged an apprenticeship for him at the Joseph Ronai Tailoring Shop, where he would learn to sew clothing and become a professional tailor. The training required one day a week in classes and four days working at the factory. After learning the rules, Siegfried explained, "I'm a Seventh-day Adventist, so I won't be able to work on Saturdays."

"That's all right," the manager said. "We'll just extend your training time by six months." But Siegfried found it so hard to remember the steps for sewing a pair of slacks and suit coats that the manager suggested he quit, believing Siegfried would never make it as a tailor. *Papa always says I'm a dummy. He must be right.* However, Mutti convinced the manager to let her son complete the course.

While traveling by bus or in the subway to deliver suits to clients, he wrote reports. Often his customers would offer him a cigarette for a tip, but he always declined. After refusing, the same customers would often give him a large cash tip.

Requirements for graduation included making a complete suit—including pants, vest, and coat—without assistance, plus pass a government examination. Soon after his 18th birthday, Siegfried told his parents, "The government has awarded me a Journeyman's License!"

Thrilled for her son, Mutti said, "You see, it pays to stick with it!" But Papa grumbled, "Why didn't you do something to earn money like your brother?" Johannes worked in the local mines and always brought home good money. But Siegfried felt perplexed by his father's comment, especially since he gave all the money he earned to support the household. *Why does he always put me down?* With graduation behind him, though, he started paying his parents 25 marks a week for room and board.

Siegfried's first job was at a small sewing shop making women's jackets. He enjoyed the work and the good pay. However, after a few pay periods, the manager told him, "Siegfried, we like your work, but you're making too much money for an 18-year-old." She then refused to pay him the wages he'd already earned.

Angry, Siegfried took the woman to the Labor Board and successfully sued to have his wages paid to him. But working there became such a miserable experience that he simply quit. Out of work, he found it very hard to find another job. So finding nothing, he said, "Goodbye Berlin," and hitchhiked deeper into West Germany, where he searched for work in Freiburg, located in the Black Forest. Every shop at which he sought work, however, always had the same problem: "Sorry, we don't hire Protestants from the North. We're all Roman Catholics." He suffered the same fate when he traveled to Offenburg. One shopkeeper there even said, "It doesn't matter how good you are, we don't hire Protestants."

Siegfried wondered how he would ever make a living—first it was age discrimination, and then it was religious discrimination. *I need money to stay alive!*

Desperate, Siegfried moved on to Frankfort and still no success. He was almost out of money and didn't know where he might stay. So he went to the home of a local pastor and explained his situation. "Sorry, we have company and no empty beds," the pastor explained. "Here's five marks. Take it and go stay in a hotel."

Uneasy with the idea of begging for a place to stay, Siegfried held onto the money and found a park bench to sleep on. The next morning, his bones ached and a stranger approached him quickly. "What are you doing here?"

"I've just come from Berlin to look for work," he answered nervously. "I don't want to spend the little money I have left on a hotel."

"Listen, young man," the stranger warned. "You better get out of here right now. This is a very dangerous part of the city." Now even more worried, Siegfried hitchhiked to Essen and started visiting every tailor shop he could find. Eventually, one kind man gave him a job. Yet not long after, he realized the suit he'd been working on had something terribly wrong with it. The owner looked over the failed project and, seeing that the sleeves were an inch too long, said. "You've done a fine job, but we are going to have to let you go. We need an experienced tailor."

Siegfried felt his stomach turning inside out. *I'm fired; what am I going to do now?* At the end of his rope, he immediately started job-hunting once more.

When asked where he came from, Siegfried never mentioned that he'd been fired from his last job. Instead, he'd simply say, "I'm from Berlin, where I recently graduated as a custom tailor." The same evening he was fired, he found a tailor shop operated out of the home of a physically handicapped owner. "You can work for me," he said, "but you will have to go out and get orders."

"How can I do that?" Siegfried was no salesman, having never successfully sold anything in his life. But he also had been praying for a job, so he felt he needed to give it his best try.

The owner handed his new employee a set of sample material and pictures showing different styles of suits. "Take these and visit the local coal miners. Find out what they like and quote a price." God blessed his work, and orders increased fast enough to keep Siegfried and his employer busy. The money he earned made it possible for him give tithe and offering to the local church and pay for board and room with a Christian family, the Vouttas.

The Vouttas and their teenage daughter, Helga, accepted Siegfried as part of the family. He attended church with them and especially enjoyed the Sabbath dinners. He loved Frau Voutta's cooking, especially her pea soup and German bread.

A young member of the Essen Adventist Church approached Siegfried. "I like your voice. Why don't you sing in the city choir.

I'll introduce you to the director." Siegfried agreed to try, and he was approved. After several months practice, he took part in a grand concert singing Brahm's "Requiem." His 100-voice choir was joined by a 200-voice boy's ensemble and five opera singers. Siegfried got goose bumps every time they sang.

On weekdays, instead of riding the streetcar to return from work, he always walked home. This saved money and gave him a chance to pick up pieces of coal that fell from mining trucks. He used the coal to keep his room warm on cold winter nights.

Then late in 1953, Siegfried received a letter from Mutti that concerned him. "Please come home immediately. Don't let anyone, especially your communist boss, know your reason for going home." *Why does she say that?* Yet even without a reason, the always obedient son left the next morning even though he hadn't worked long enough to earn vacation pay.

He only lacked two weeks of service, but his boss gave him a firm, "No!" when he asked to receive the vacation pay. So to save money, he decided to hitchhike to Berlin. On the way, a man in a black Mercedes picked him up. As the car sped along the icy autobahn, Siegfried prayed, "Dear Lord, please keep us safe." Still speeding, the driver reached into the glove compartment and pulled out a revolver. *Why is he showing me this?!* Yet the Lord answered his prayers, as the man returned the weapon into the glove compartment and dropped him off at the East German border.

Siegfried walked across the Russian Border Control and caught a bus all the way to Berlin. He had lived away from home for over a year and the thought of seeing his parents made his heart beat fast. He walked through the garden gate to the house longing to see Papa and Muti. Greeting his parents, he asked, "Why did you have me rush home on such short notice?"

"Well, son, Berlin is just a little island in a big communist world." His father explained that the Russians continued to break agreements with the Allies, recalling when they'd stopped all rail, water, and highway transportation through East Germany to West Berlin. The communists had hoped that the West would leave Berlin so they could take over, but their hopes disintegrated when the West organized the Berlin Airlift. Planes carrying supplies arrived as often as one every minute. More than 250,000 flights helped save the people from starvation and ruin. "But we don't know what the Russians will do next," his father lamented. "The future here seems very uncertain."

Siegfried recalled the roar of airplanes taking off and pilots tossing packets of raisins or candy from the cockpit. Children even began referring to the planes as raisin bombers. He asked, "So what are you planning to do?"

"More and more restrictions are being placed on travel," Papa answered. "We want to immigrate to America before it's too late."

"The United States?" Siegfried listened in astonishment. He'd been taught to be unquestionably patriotic during his time at a Hitler Youth Camp, and so he had never thought about leaving Germany.

"We want you to go with us," his parents insisted.

"What about Johannes? Is he going too?" Siegfried asked.

"We want him to go. His documentation is ready, but it's up to him. He's chosen a different lifestyle and has a girlfriend, so we're not sure."

Then Mutti explained, "We've worked for months to get our documents in order. We just lack one thing. We need someone in America to guarantee us. We're not asking for money or tickets. All we need is a signature to make our immigration legal. I have a letter ready to mail."

"Siegfried," she continued. "I know you are tired after your long trip, but this is urgent. Will you ride your bike to the airport so the letter can go out on the next flight?" Siegfried pedaled his bicycle eight miles to the airport. As he dropped the letter into the airmail slot, he wondered if the trouble was worth all the effort.

The letter from the Neuendorffs fell into the hands of a German pastor before the next weekend. On that Sabbath, he read it to the congregation at the Loma Linda Campus Hill Church. One family there was impressed to give the family the much-needed guarantee.

Before long, the Neuendorffs began finalizing plans, thrilled at the prospect of living in a free country with many more opportunities for a better life. It seemed to them that the Lord was blessing them, as their house and furniture sold in record time, which helped them earn enough money to cover their travel expenses. With passports and visas in hand, they were ready to go.

Unwilling to risk traveling through the Russian-occupied zone, they chartered a flight to Hamburg. At the airport, Johannes showed up intoxicated from a night of drinking. Sadly, the family had to leave him behind. "Don't worry," Papa said. "He can come later."

As the plane climbed off the tarmac, Siegfried looked out the window. *Goodbye Berlin! This is the city where I was born.* He'd spent much of his childhood watching Berlin burn. It's where his family survived a terrible war. *Thank you, God.* It's even where I learned my trade.

Eventually, the city vanished from sight. His mind wandered to how his mother helped lead him to Christ. He remembered too that he had promised on the day of his baptism to be faithful to God. *Dear Lord, please help keep that promise as I start a new life in America.*

The plane landed in Hamburg, and after clearing customs and immigration, the family purchased bus tickets to Bremerhaven. *My family is on its way to a new world. What plans does God have for me? What will my future be like?* Soon they arrived at the port, where Siegfried was amazed at the incredible vessel that would carry them across an ocean.

Their economy tickets put them in a cabin on the bottom deck of the *SS United States.* On the way in the North Atlantic, a winter storm pummeled the ship. Waves up to 50-feet high crashed over the bow. Papa said, "It doesn't make a difference if you're in a luxury suite or in economy—everybody's seasick."

Papa and Mutti were miserable for the entire crossing. Like most other passengers, they stayed in their cabin. But Siegfried braved the rough conditions, venturing out for meals and walking the deck as the ship tossed around the ocean like a toy.

But nearly six days after leaving Bremerhaven, the family stood on the deck, fascinated by the New York skyline. They'd read about this city, but now they could see it with their own eyes. The giant ship made it's way past the Statue of Liberty as Siegfried looked on and wondered. What will America be like?

They'd prayed for this experience. Now they feared an uncertain future.

Chapter 4
Rich Man's Welcome

~~~~~~~~~~

S iegfried wished for more time to see New York, but the Neuendorff family was on a tight schedule. Hailing a taxi at the port, they rushed to the airport and arrived just in time to board the shiny American Airlines DC-6 that would take them to Los Angeles on the other side of America.

Will California be like the garden of Eden? Siegfried had heard glowing descriptions of the land out west, full of wealth. He wondered if their sponsor was rolling in money. With a name like Richman, Siegfried figured, He's got to be rich.

Huge crowds at the L.A. Airport didn't keep Mr. Richman from spotting the Neuendorffs immediately. Everything about them shouted foreigners—from their clothing, hairstyles, shoes, even the way they walked. The short, gray-haired sponsor introduced himself. With very little knowledge of English, about all Neuendorffs could do was say, "Hello."

While Mr. Richman led them to the parking lot, Siegfried wondered what kind of car he'd be driving. He eyed the rickety old gray Ford as Mr. Richman loaded their bags into the back. As they drove off, the doors rattled and the windows wouldn't shut properly. *He probably owns a California gold mine. He's just playing a trick on us.* Siegfried imagined it might be some kind of test, and that Mr. Richman had a nice Cadillac parked in his garage at home.

As they took off down the San Bernardino Freeway, Siegfried tried to use the few English words he'd learned from American troops occupying West Berlin. Papa and Mutti were overwhelmed by all the lights as they drove over Kellogg Hill through Pomona, Ontario, Fontana, Rialto, and Colton. After nearly two hours driving, Mr. Richman pointed to the right. "That's Loma Linda," he said. "We're going to turn left."

There were no streetlights when they turned onto Davidson Street. Everything was dark as they passed a few houses and finally turned left onto the Richman property. The land was strewn with worn-out refrigerators and several beat up old cars. *This man sure likes Fords.* Siegfried also saw two donkeys walking around. *Perhaps he owns a Lincoln.*

A mangy dog yapped at the family as they entered the house. There were no curtains on the windows or locks on the doors, not even on the bathroom door. They stared in amazement. Siegfried whispered to his parents, "Why did you bring me here? Our house in Berlin's better than this!"

For supper they were served avocados, cottage cheese, and bread with caraway seed. They'd never tasted any of these before, but they were too tired to really care. All three of them were exhausted from the endless days of travel, and they hadn't slept well for days because of the Atlantic storm.

Mrs. Richman asked the three of them to share one double bed. Although Siegfried fell asleep immediately, Mutti cried, "Is this what America's all about? What have we gotten ourselves into?" Unable to really sleep, his parents struggled to get to breakfast in the morning, where they were served cornflakes and oranges. They had never heard of cornflakes, and oranges were a luxury they only enjoyed at Christmas.

Before driving to Loma Linda, Mr. Richman explained his work plan for the new family. Walter was to repair the house and work in the yard, and his son would help. Mutti would do the housework and cooking for the Richman family. Your food and lodging will be free, and I'll give the three of you $50 a month that you can share.

Siegfried gulped. *We're worth a lot more than this! This isn't right.* His father was thinking the same, and spoke out when they were alone in the bedroom. "We've paid our own way. I don't think it's right for us to have to work for such low wages. The agenda will have to change."

So while in Loma Linda, Mr. Richman introduced the Neuendorffs to Louise Scholz, an elderly German lady who'd served 16 years as a missionary in India. Mutti erupted, "It's so wonderful to have someone to speak German with."

Amazingly, Louise asked, "Why don't you stay with me?"

Papa and Mutti discussed the options of staying with her or returning home to the sponsor. It was hardly a difficult choice, as they wouldn't have to share a bed with Siegfried and they'd have a person nearby who spoke German.

"Mr. Richman," they explained, "Your guarantee was an answer to prayer. We appreciate your kindness to us. This lady just invited us to stay with her now, and since she speaks German, we think that will be best." Mr. Richman seemed disappointed, but he agreed to take them to pick up the things they'd left at his home.

⁓

Lodging at Louise Scholz's house lasted just one night however. An animal lover, she took care of five small dogs and eleven cats. The odor was more than the guest family could handle. Despite the wonderful hospitality, they had to find another place to go.

Two German women learned of their plight and let the family spend a couple of nights in their home. Another German family, the Steinmanns then offered to let them stay at their place a few days until they could find something permanent.

One of Steinmann's daughters, Maja, owned her own car. "Siegfried," she asked one day, "Would you like to drive?" Stunned by the offer, he barely trusted his ears. *Did I hear that correctly?* Siegfried had been in a car only a few times in his life. Most of his transportation had been by bicycle. Now he was asked if he wanted to actually drive one!

Flabbergasted, Siegfried blurted out, "I'd sure like to try." Maja drove him out to a nearby orange grove. She explained how to turn the key to start the engine, turn the steering wheel, step on the throttle, and use the brakes. Finally, Siegfried, feeling shaky, climbed in the driver's seat. It was an amazing feeling to be behind the wheel, and after a successful drive around the grove, he shouted, "Hello, America! I go for this! Wow!"

A few days later, the family rented a room at the Loma Linda Sanitarium building where all three could stay for $15 a month. It certainly was a bargain, but there was only one problem: Rent has to be paid in advance and all they had was a credit check for $20 from an airline.

As his parents tried to decide what to do, Siegfried volunteered, "I'll hitchhike to Los Angeles and cash the check." So early the next morning, Siegfried stood out on the highway trying to flag down a car. A driver pulled over and let him in, then sped out of the city. On the way, the driver reached into the glove box to show Siegfried a pistol.

What is going on? It was the exact thing that happened to him as he hitchhiked to Berlin. Only 12 miles down the road, the driver dropped him off by a grape vineyard near Cucamonga. A truck collecting used oil from service stations picked him up. Learning Siegfried's dilemma, the driver said, "If you'll stay with me while I do my work, I'll take you to downtown Los Angeles.

"Sure, I'll stay with you," Siegfried agreed. *I'd have a hard time finding the airline office by myself.* Later that day, Siegfried cashed the check, and then the truck driver took him all the way back to Loma Linda. That evening, he told his parents what a complete stranger had done for him. Then he asked, "Is this what Americans are like all the time?" Full of joy, he answered his own question, "They're wonderful!" The next day the family paid for a month's rent and moved into the Loma Linda Sanitarium. "God is looking out for us," Siegfried declared.

Mutti got a housekeeping job at the Loma Linda Hospital for a dollar an hour. Papa earned two dollars an hour at a Fontana cabinet shop. And a student at La Sierra College offered to teach Siegfried how to nail rock lath. He would earn 45 cents for every bundle he nailed to walls.

Should be simple enough; I know how to use a needle and thread. But at first, having a mouth full of blue nails and using a hammer to drive them into the wall was a much more difficult challenged than he imagined. But it wasn't long until he got so good at it that he was making more money than his dad.

The Neuendorffs thanked God for making it possible for them to be self-supporting from the very beginning of their experience in a new country. The family of three, instead of earning 50 dollars a month, was now bringing in more than 50 dollars a day. They moved out of their old room and rented an apartment on Loma Linda's Barton Road.

In Southern California, Siegfried found himself in need of a car. He couldn't jump on a streetcar like he did back in Berlin, so he needed to find a way to get to his lathing jobs. He offered to buy an old 1942 Dodge if he could pass a driving test. With the little English he knew, he studied hard and walked away from the Department of Vehicles with his new driver's license.

As a Berliner, he loved driving his own car and earning American money, but he also felt so out of place pounding thousands of blue lathing nails every day. *I don't like having my mouth full of nails. What if swallow one?*

Not long after, a church member told him about a job at Tailored Slacks in Rialto, only nine miles from Loma Linda. Located in a large industrial complex, the company hired 200 women seamstresses and six men as designers or cutters.

Siegfried, familiar with industrial sewing machines, was hired to be the sleeve setter. He remembered that back in Berlin, he lost his first job because he messed up on the sleeves. He'd worked extra hard to make sure it wouldn't happen like that again.

His job was a blessing to him. *I feel like a prince!* Everyone treated him with patience as he struggled to learn English. On his birthday, the women at the factory even gave him a spotlight for his car.

In a very little time, Siegfried had become an incredibly hard worker. Beginning at 7:00 A.M., he worked an eight-hour shift setting sleeves. He then drove to a lathing site and worked two hours, and after that he worked at a Shell station in Redlands where he serviced cars and repaired tires until 10:00. Mutti encouraged her son. "I know you are working long days, but at least you are getting ahead financially." And along the way, to learn more English, he would read volumes in spite of all the work he was doing.

By the end of the year, he was able to purchase a brand-new black 1954 Volkswagen Beetle. It caused a stir in his neighborhood in Southern California, where few had ever seen a car with an air-cooled engine mounted in the rear.

⁓

Without giving it much thought, Siegfried had joined the Amalgamated Clothing Workers of America to get his tailoring job.

It shocked him to read publications about the labor union's strong-arm tactics that didn't seem compatible with biblical standards.

On evening he told his parents, "For conscience sake, I'm quitting the union. Labor unions may accomplish some good, but the means used to reach their goals are not right. I must please Christ before I please my company."

Papa questioned, "Aren't you getting fanatical."

"No, Papa. It's not fanatical. It's pleasing Jesus. God will forgive me for the past because I didn't know better. Scripture says, 'Times of ignorance God overlooked' (Acts 17:30). Since I've seen the light, I must be true to my convictions."

Siegfried's break with the union soon had him labeled as a troublemaker. Yet the company desperately needed his skill, so they let him continue working anyway. Before long, the foreman announced, "Beginning with the next pay period, everyone will go on piecework." For Siegfried, it was great news since he was working so fast now.

He asked the foreman, "How much will you pay for each set of sleeves in boy's coats?"

The foreman responded, "Nine cents per coat."

Siegfried smiled in disbelief. "You must be kidding! Laughing, Siegfried sarcastically added, "That's too much money!" But in seriousness, Siegfried knew he couldn't work for so little. The sleeve is the only part of a garment that doesn't have just a straight seam and flat material. It's curved and it takes experience and technique to sew a sleeve on a jacket. So although he had never missed a day of work, he stayed home the next day. Four women struggled to do the work he'd done by himself.

Two days later, the assistant manager showed up at Siegfried's apartment. "We want you to come back," he said.

"Not for that kind of pay," Siegfried objected.

"Well, how much do you want?"

"Fifteen cents per set of sleeves, and no less."

"That's six cents more than the union proposal?" Yet it didn't matter; they needed his skill. "Come back tomorrow and we'll give you what you're asking for. But don't tell anyone about our agreement."

Siegfried agreed and went back to work, but two weeks later he received a paycheck that showed he'd only been paid 12 cents a sleeve. *What a disappointment! Should I quit?* However, he reasoned that even with less pay, he was still making good money and it was a steady job.

As the clothing factory's success greatly increased the workload and more orders were coming in, the assistant manager asked Siegfried, "To keep up, we want you to work on Saturdays."

"I'm sorry, sir," Siegfried explained. "I believe in the Sabbath. If I truly love Jesus, I must obey His commandment and rest from sundown Friday until sundown on Saturday. The Sabbath is a special day of worship, and I will not work that day."

"What kind of a man are you, Neuendorff? We stuck our necks out for you by not firing you after you left the union. Now you want to make it difficult for us and refuse to work on Saturdays?"

"Sir," Siegfried answered. "I'll be glad to work all day on Sundays, but I can never work on God's Sabbath!" Because of the need to keep production going, the man agreed. "I'll come every Sunday and open up this big building and lock you in. You can work all day without interruptions. I'll be back in the afternoons to let you out."

The plan worked well until a union representative discovered the arrangement and blew up. "They're opening this huge industrial complex just for you on Sundays, and they're paying more than the union approved. It's illegal, and it's got to stop!"

To avoid causing further problems, Siegfried resigned the next day. Looking back, he knew it was providential for him to be fired for failing to get the sleeves right on my first job in the city of Essen. It helped him put more effort to get things right. Siegfried determined not to let this setback hurt him financially. *I'll just go out and get more lathing jobs. I hate nails in my mouth, but it pays well and there's lots of construction going on.*

I'm sure God has a plan for my life.

Chapter 5
Greetings from the President

The President of the United States—
Greetings: You are hereby ordered to report to the Local Board [132 located at the] AMERICAN LEGION POST 14, 386 Fourth Street, San Bernardino, California at 7:00 A.M. on Thursday of July 12, 1956, for forwarding to an induction station.

Although he was a German citizen living in America, Siegfried had been required to register for the draft when he arrived. He never gave it much thought until he got this letter in the mailbox. Questions he'd never had reason to think raced through his mind. *What will I do in the United States Army? What kind of food is served to soldiers?* He didn't even know if he would be able to understand orders in English. But most worrisome of all was wondering if they would let him keep the Sabbath.

He thought about not even showing up, but the thought of a $10,000 fine or a long prison sentence quickly diminished that idea. He decided to report. While registering, Siegfried declared himself a conscientious objector and received the classification I-A-O, meaning he was willing to serve his adopted country as a non-combatant, but his conscience would not allow him to take human life.

After reporting to the local board, Siegfried, along with a bus load of recruits, was driven to a processing center in Los Angeles. As men lined up for a quick health check and a battery of vaccinations an officer ordered, "Take off your clothes! Shoes, socks, underclothes, everything."

"What?" Siegfried questioned. *Isn't there any privacy at all in the U. S. Army? We were taught to be modest in the Hitler Youth Camp.* As the vaccinations were completed, a barber also clipped each soldier's hair as close to the skin as possible. Finally they were issued a uniform and told to dress. Siegfried looked around the room and studied every one standing there. *We all look alike!*

Instead of pledging, "I hereby promise to defend the USA and its constitution by *all* means," non-combatants, classified as I-A-O, took a different oath of induction: "I hereby promise to defend the USA and its constitution by all *justifiable* means."

All the willing combatants were shipped immediately to Fort Ord in California for training, while Siegfried and other I-A-Os were sent to Fort Sam Houston in San Antonio, Texas, for training as medics. As conscientious cooperators, they would be trained only to save human life.

Siegfried found inspiration in the life of Desmond Doss, a conscientious objector during World War II who received a purple heart for saving lives on the front lines. During the long trip to Fort Sam Houston, a Bible verse grabbed his attention. "You … must endure hardship as a good soldier of Jesus Christ" (2 Timothy 2:3). *With Christ's help,* Siegfried determined, *I will not assimilate the customary swearing and vulgarities so often found in the Army. My thoughts and words must be always pure. I will always ask the blessing on my food before eating. I will kneel and pray the first thing in the morning and before I go to sleep at night.*

He also resolved to make time to study his Bible. *And whatever it costs, I will honor the Creator by observing the holy Sabbath.*

On his first Sabbath at Fort Sam Houston, Siegfried found a group of Adventists worshiping in the chapel. As a newcomer to the group, they asked him to pray. Embarrassed because he'd never prayed in English, he stumbled through a simple prayer. But he felt accepted by his fellow soldiers in the chapel that day anyway.

Basic training didn't exactly fit Siegfried's independent personality. He recalled the military discipline he had received at the Hitler Youth Camp in Poland. More than ever, he found himself disliking being called out of bed by a whistle and ordered around by the shrill voice of a shouting Sergeant. *Why do they make us do push-ups on an empty stomach?*

He was annoyed how much they treated him like a toddler. *They tell us how to handle a broom, use a mop, and even how to lace our boots.* He resented being told what to do and how to do it every minute of the day. *Why do they rush us from one place to another only to stand for hours?*

One day they were ordered to enter a gas chamber, remove their gas mask, and put it on again. The men coughed while tears flooded their eyes. Fumes burned their lungs. Immediately they were ordered out to crawl over an obstacle course of Texas rocks while bullets were fired over their heads. "You men will be providing medical care in these conditions, so you need to learn to protect yourselves now," they were told. But Siegfried did love some parts of training, like when they had him practice driving a Jeep in rugged terrain.

After a few days in basic training, a Right Guide was chosen for each platoon. The Guide's responsibilities included waking the men in the morning and marching them to the mess hall and classes. The man chosen for his platoon abused his authority by leaving his men standing in the hot sun on several occasions. The soldiers rebelled and asked for a new Right Guide.

The First Sergeant called the men to stand in formation. "Who's had military training?" he asked. At first no one spoke up. Then someone shouted, "Neuendorff! He trained as a Hitler Youth." Someone else added. "He also attended the Desmond Doss Medical Cadet Corp Camp in Michigan."

After a unanimous vote, the Sergeant turned to Siegfried, "You've got the job."

Siegfried couldn't believe it. Not only was he not a U.S. citizen, he struggled with English and knew that most of the men were much more educated than he was. Still, he determined as always to do his best.

All of the men were classified as conscientious objectors. Some were Bible-believing Christians, but many others who did not believe in God were also convicted it's wrong to take another human's life.

Others were simply troublemakers. They often made fun of Siegfried's accent, always imitating him when he called out, "Platoon, fall out!" At six-feet, four-inches tall, he had the advantage of being the tallest, which gave him the ability to handle tense situations with authority. By being kind and firm, and taking teasing with a smile, he formed a strong bond with the twenty-seven men in his platoon.

⁓

After eight weeks of basic training, the platoon was given two-weeks leave to visit their families. Desperate to get home cheaply, Siegfried found an agency in San Antonio looking for drivers to deliver cars to the West Coast. He chose a black Volkswagen convertible.

Driving through a small town in Arizona, Siegfried looked in his rearview mirror after glancing a bright red light flash. A police car pulled in behind him, so he pulled off the road and came to a stop.

The highway patrol officer reached his window. "I have to write you up, young man, for doing 75 in a 55-mile zone. "

"But Sir," Siegfried pleaded, "I've just finished the first eight weeks of basic training. A traffic ticket will ruin my record."

"Listen, soldier, this is Arizona. You've messed up your record!" The officer paused and looked strait into Siegfried's eyes. "I appreciate what young men like you do for our country, but the law is the law."

"I understand," Siegfried answered.

The officer smiled, "Promise me that you won't drive over the speed limit in Arizona, and I'll tear up your citation!"

"Sir, I promise. Thank you for your kindness." Siegfried kept that promise all the way to California.

At home, Siegfried praised his mother after the tasting the food he so missed. "Mutti, your cooking's never tasted better. It's great to be with you and Papa."

However, thinking about her son's future, she said, "I'm glad you like my food, but some day you'll need your own cook. By the time you get out of the army, you'll be too old to live at home."

"Mutti, what are you trying to say?"

"Three years ago I met a student nurse from Canada. She treated me kindly and spoke in German. She's graduated from nursing and works at the Loma Linda Hospital. I want you to meet her."

"I like girls, Mom, but I don't want to get involved right now." He put the whole thing out of his mind.

Four days before returning to the army base in Texas, Mutti said, "Papa needs you to drive him to Redlands to pick up his car. You could go by Loma Linda on the way and meet the girl I've been telling you about."

"No way!"

"But, Siegfried, I told her you'd be coming."

"You should have asked me first!" Upset but obedient, Siegfried soon relented. *Why am I doing this?* He knocked on the door of the nurse's apartments on Mound Street in Loma Linda. *What will she look like? What can I say?*

The door opened, and Siegfried stood stunned. Evelyn Trupp, a five-foot-four beauty with dark brown hair and bright blue eyes smiled. Regaining composure, he blurted, "I'm taking my father to Redlands to pick up a car. Would you like to go along?"

"Sure," she said. "I'll be glad to get away from Loma Linda for a little while."

They dropped Papa off at the auto repair. Siegfried thought the drive to Redlands had been too short, so he determined to go a longer way home to Loma Linda, by Timothy Canyon Road. There was no way a policeman would pull him over for a speeding ticket this time.

The two enjoyed conversing in German and discovered they had a lot of common interests. Reaching the apartment building, Siegfried said, "It's been great visiting with you. I just wish I didn't have to return to Texas in four days."

"Listen, Siegfried," Evelyn smiled. "I'm off work tomorrow—I can take the next day off too." The two then spent as much time as they were able getting to know each other a lot better.

Yet all too soon, they were saying goodbye—but with a promise, "We'll keep in touch!" Heading back to Texas, Siegfried couldn't think of anything else but Evelyn. *When will I see her again? Is she the one God wants for me?*

Back at the base, he waited two weeks before writing. Evelyn waited another two weeks to answer. Soon they were writing more frequently, and she often sent cassettes with poetry or music. She was becoming more attractive every day. *What a morale booster for a lonely soldier.*

Siegfried's platoon buddies voted for him to continue as Right Guide during their final eight weeks of training. "You've helped us work together as a team," they said.

Siegfried soon got word that he was going to Fort Lewis, Washington. This typically meant that he would be processed and shipped to South Korea. *I want to go to Europe, not the Far East!*

Siegfried called his parents. "Please contact the German Church in Los Angeles and ask them to pray that if it's the Lord's will, I can be reassigned to Europe." Evelyn began to pray too. Then Siegfried went from officer to officer. "What can I do to get my orders changed?"

The response was always the same. "Impossible! You are on the list, and no exceptions will be made."

Siegfried prayed earnestly, "Lord, you know what's best. If you want me to go to Europe, please open the way." The last day at Fort Sam Houston arrived and Siegfried's platoon stood in formation. One by one, the Captain called each soldier by name and serial number. The majority of the men were heading to Fort Lewis. Siegfried agonized. *Will God answer my prayer?*

Finally the Captain called, "Neuendorff, front and center!" Siegfried stepped forward, stood at attention, and saluted. The Captain lowered his voice, "I'm sorry." He hesitated. "I'm sorry to tell you, we are sending you to Fort Dix in New Jersey."

"Hurrah!" Siegfried shouted. "This means I'm going to Europe. God answers prayer!" His platoon cheered. Excited, he grabbed his orders from the captain's hand, turned, and fell back into rank.

On the train heading to Fort Dix that evening, Siegfried mused. *It's strange to be traveling with a bunch of soldiers I've never seen before. What does the Lord have in mind for me now?* He also thought about Evelyn. *We've been writing almost every day. When will I see her again?*

The routine at Fort Dix turned into a waiting game. After several days of waiting for orders, Siegfried heard he would be stationed in Hanau, Germany. It was only 11 miles from Frankfurt, the place where he had slept on a park bench to save money.

An announcement over a loudspeaker on Friday ordered Siegfried's group of solders to be at the bus stop the next morning. They would be taken to the port for boarding a troop transport ship. Saturday morning, Siegfried and his group stood with their duffel bags waiting for the bus. Troubled thoughts raced through his mind. *This is God's Sabbath. It's not a day to travel. What shall I do?*

He breathed a silent prayer as a big green military bus screeched to a stop. Men entered the bus as their names were called. More and more names, but Siegfried didn't hear his. Finally, only four men stood in line. The driver shouted, "You men aren't on the list. Go back to your barracks and wait for orders."

Siegfried spent a quiet Sabbath reading his Bible, praying, and thanking God for keeping him from traveling on Sabbath. *Does this mean I won't be going to Germany after all?*

Four frustrating days later, he heard his name and serial number 56278975 along with many others. "Report to the bus station in the morning. You will be taken to a military airport here in New Jersey and flown to Frankfurt, Germany, after a stopover in the Azores.

"Wonderful!" Siegfried exclaimed. "God did it again. He worked things out better than I could imagine." He was assigned to the 7th Army, 36th Medical Battalion, Medical Company 429. That night he dreamed of meeting relatives and old friends back in Germany.

Flying over the Atlantic the next day, his thoughts turned to Loma Linda and the lovely blue-eyed nurse with the dark brown hair. *Will she keep writing when I'm so far away*

⌒

Arriving in Hanau two days before Christmas, his first tasks included cleaning medical instruments, painting trucks, going on maneuvers, and accepting special assignments.

The men in his squad complained when they were forced to pitch tents and set up a medical field station at 3:00 in the morning.

Weather conditions on one maneuver were so bad that tanks, trucks, and even a tank retriever got stuck in the mud. Ambulances were unable to move in what they called the *Battle of Mud*.

Siegfried, impressed by words of Jesus, "If you love Me, keep My commandments" (John 14:15), determined that he would always honor the Savior with his language. Men poked fun at him for not swearing. He soon noticed, though, that when he came around someone would say, "Stop cussing; Neuendorff's here."

Because of the command, "You shall not kill," Siegfried entered the service as a conscientious objector. When the a sergeant insisted he work in the weapons room, he responded, "Sir, I want to do all I can to support the government, but my conscience does not allow me to bear arms."

Later, the same Sergeant offered him an easy job. "All you have to do is pick up the mail on Saturday mornings and deliver it to the men. Don't tell me you can't do that either?"

Siegfried smiled, "Sergeant, that's when I go to church." He believed that Jesus wrote with his own finger on a table of stone: "Remember the Sabbath day, to keep it holy. Six days you shall labor and do all your work, but the seventh day is the Sabbath of the LORD your God. In it you shall do no work. … for in six days the LORD made the heavens and the earth, the sea, and all that is in them, and rested the seventh day. Therefore the LORD blessed the Sabbath day and hallowed it" (Exodus 20:8-11).

The Sergeant yelled, "Neuendorff, you're useless in our company!" For not attending a 20-minute police call to pick up papers and cigarette butts on another Sabbath, he had to spend all day Sunday cleaning bathrooms, washing windows, watering flowers, and painting a truck. He kept smiling, but even his buddies said, "This is an injustice."

Not long after, a more disturbing order came. "Medical Battalion 36 will spend Friday, Saturday, Sunday, and Monday practicing war games." *Now what will I do? The Holy Sabbath is not a day to practice war games.* Siegfried invited another Adventist medic to his room. They closed the door and prayed together. "Dear God, please help find a solution."

Early Friday morning, on the day the maneuvers were to begin, the Battalion Commander, Captain Smith, announced,

"Headquarters and Ambulance Companies will go out, but Medical Company will stay in the barracks."

What? This makes no sense! What will Headquarters Company have to report if the medics don't bring any patients? And will the ambulances just drive around in empty vehicles?

With two companies out on maneuvers, Friday afternoon proved very quiet at the base. Siegfried started washing an old 1941 VW he'd just purchased. Nearby, the captain washed his 220 Mercedes Benz.

Siegfried walked up to the captain and saluted. "Sir, I'm puzzled. Why didn't we go on maneuvers today? The captain responded curtly. "I cancelled your company's going out."

"But why, Captain? The order came from the 7th Army in Frankfurt."

"Neuendorff, I felt your company had no need to go out. Why are you asking?"

"Captain, you know I'm a Seventh-day Adventist Christian. I didn't feel it would be right to be out on the field on Sabbath, so I prayed God would find a way out."

"Neuendorff, consider this as an answer to your prayer."

"Thank you, Sir, for your part in solving my predicament."

While continuing to wash his old Volkswagon, Siegfried lifted his heart to heaven. "Thank you, Lord, for touching the captain's heart so I could honor another Sabbath."

Serving in the army in Germany revived memories of his days as a Hitler youth. *I got into serious trouble for refusing to eat a fish without fins and scales, but the Lord solved the problem.* He'd also been reading that a vegetarian diet led to healthy bodies and even aided in a person's spiritual life. A growing conviction led him to decide to give up on meat in his diet. *From now on, I will be a vegetarian.*

⟨⁓⟩

Two weeks later, his company spent three weekdays on maneuvers—the only food: C-rations giving a choice of pork and beans or chicken and noodles plus dessert. *I'm not going back to eating meat,* he determined. *I've made up my mind.* He survived the next three days eating crackers and jam with a little milk. Although it was a very unbalanced diet, he stood firm.

When the men in Siegfried's company were given a week's leave, Siegfried decided to visit his old home in Berlin. To avoid traveling through the Russian zone, he flew. *If the Russians catch a Berliner in a U. S. Army uniform, I could be in real trouble.*

On Sabbath, he was welcomed by members at the church he joined by baptism when he was 13. Seeing friends from the war years brought tears of joy. *I'm so thankful that the Holy Spirit impressed me to dedicate my life to Jesus while I was still young.*

Visiting the old home where his family survived years of fiery bombs during Allied raids made him appreciate, more than ever, the divine protection that kept him safe when so many others died. *God must have a special plan for me.*

Life back at the barracks in Hanau did not provide an atmosphere for Christian growth. Buddies harassed him constantly. "Man, you're an odd ball," they taunted. "You won't drink, you don't smoke, you don't swear, you don't dance, and now this crazy idea—you won't eat meat!

Siegfried listened as the men continued. "Where's your masculinity? You won't chase women on the street or sleep with a prostitute. Are you a real man? Can't you have a little fun?"

"Listen, fellows. Yes, I'm a man and plan to marry some day. I want to be worthy of a good wife. I want to be able to look her in the eyes and say, 'You're the only one.' " While his buddies caroused in bars and chased women, Siegfried stayed in the barracks. He studied for his GED test, wrote letters to the nurse in Loma Linda, and spent time doing needlework that he'd learned as a tailor.

Each time he watched servicemen line up for penicillin shots to combat gonorrhea and syphilis, he thanked God for inspired counsel found in the Bible. "Flee sexual immorality" (1 Corinthians 6:18). *The Christian really has the advantage.*

Every letter from Evelyn was also giving Siegfried greater conviction. *With Christ's help, I'll keep myself pure. I will not sin against God.*

While tormenting Siegfried for being different, servicemen still showed respect and trust for a man with courage to stand up for what he believed. They often left their money with him because they didn't want to lose their wallets while intoxicated.

Another advantage: While the majority spent their money on weekends, Siegfried saved his. A few months before completing his tour in Germany, he ordered a Mercedes Benz 180 D directly from the factory in Stuttgart. *Since my buddies constantly poke fun at me, how will they react when I drive my new car back to the base?*

Chapter 6
The Answer Is "Yes"

Siegfried ripped open the latest letter from Loma Linda. "What's it like in Germany?" He wasted no time to answer.

"Dear, Evelyn," he wrote. "Why don't you come and find out for yourself." *She'll never do it.*

A few weeks later, Evelyn purchased a round-trip ticket to Germany. Siegfried met her at the Frankfurt airport and with quivering hands handed her a bouquet of red roses. An elderly lady in the Hanau church offered her a place to stay. On weekends they attended the local church or drove to the Adventist Servicemen's Center in Frankfurt.

Evelyn told him that a nurse friend was coming and they were going to do some traveling together. The two nurses rented a car and drove to the Black Forest in Southern Germany. After a few days, Siegfried began calling the home where she stayed. "Are the ladies back yet?"

"No," was the answer from the elderly lady.

Another day he called. "No." He couldn't take the wait any longer.

But finally, "Yes, they just arrived."

He asked to speak with Evelyn. "I'd like to come pick you up this evening and take you to vespers at the Service Men's Center in Frankfurt."

Heading back to Hanau after the meeting, they drove along the Main River. Siegfried kept thinking, *What a lovely personality. It's wonderful to be with her.*

He slowed, turned off the road, and parked near the river. He reached for her hand. "Evelyn," he said. "We have so much in common. We were born the same year. We've both been raised in Adventist homes. We speak German." He hesitated and squeezed her hand. "Will you marry me?"

A long moment of silence followed, but with a voice full of charm she answered, "My answer is 'yes.'" They prayed together, asking God to lead in all their plans for the future.

Whether it was to become a vegetarian or get married, once a decision had been made, Siegfried was ready to act. For a soldier to marry while serving overseas, he needed permission from the Army. He went to his commanding officer and made a formal application. Without giving a reason, he was told, "Your request to marry is denied."

Forced to wait, Siegfried tried to figure out why. *I'm a German citizen serving in the U. S. Army. Evelyn's father immigrated to Canada from Southern Russia. With the tension of the Cold War, they may think our union is not appropriate at this time.*

"Evelyn," he said, "God knows what's best. I'll soon be out of the army. I'll go to Canada to meet your parents. We can have a church wedding like you want." Before going to her parents in Canada, Evelyn flew to London and visited nearby Newbold College.

Siegfried traveled to the Daimler-Benz factory in Stuttgart and picked up the car he'd ordered. Back at the barracks, his buddies ran out to look. "What a baby!" they shouted. The new light metallic blue Mercedes Benz 180 glistened in the afternoon sun. It also featured white walls, an ivory steering wheel, AM/FM radio, and reclining seats with red leatherette upholstery!

"How did you do this, Neuendorff?" one of them asked. "You're just a Specialist, 3rd Class. No soldier can afford a car like this."

"God blessed me," he declared. "I always tithe my monthly earnings and you know I haven't spent money on entertainment. I had a little savings left from the sale of a Volkswagen I owned before entering the army, and by saving my money here, it was easy to make a purchase like this."

"Neuendorff, we thought you were crazy. Looks like you're the smart one."

"I'm glad you like my car. I'm taking it to the port of Bremerhaven for shipment to New York. I'll drive to Canada where I'll be married in a church wedding to a wonderful Christian nurse. We'll take the car on our honeymoon."

Siegfried received a good conduct medal for two years of military service and letters of recommendation from two officers. For his trip back to the states, he was placed on a crowded troop ship to New York and assigned guard duty. To prevent fires on board, his job was to make sure no one smoked. The difficult part of the job was staying awake on long night shifts. Because of the miserable night guard duty, Siegfried's voyage seemed to last forever.

I've done my best to serve America. Like the first time he had first seen America's shores, he watched Statue of Liberty as the ship drew nearer. *Someday I'll become a citizen.* After receiving an honorable discharge, he set out to locate the Mercedes he'd shipped ahead. He found it on the dock—just as beautiful as the day he picked it up at the factory—and not a scratch.

"Dear God," he prayed. "Thank you for keeping me during my time in the military and for a safe trip across the Atlantic. Please lead me as I begin a new life."

The Mercedes ate up 1,600 miles of highway, reaching the Trupp farm near Winnipeg, Manitoba, in record time. After meeting them for the first time, Siegfried believed Evelyn's parents to be fine people. *No wonder their daughter has such an attractive personality.* But one thing needed to be settled.

Siegfried hesitated. *How can I do this? What if they say no?* Finally facing Evelyn's parents, he took courage. "I was impressed with your daughter the first time we met. We've been writing for almost two years. During her visit to Germany, we were convinced God wants us to spend our lives together. I'd like permission to marry Evelyn."

The Trupps laughed with joy. "We've heard a lot about you, and you have our permission." Evelyn's family helped plan the wedding. The Province of Manitoba issued the marriage license.

Papa and Muti came all the way from California, and Evelyn's family and friends were all present. The loving couple stood facing the minister in the little German Mountain View Adventist Church in Winnipeg. After declaring their love for each other, they walked down the aisle unable to imagine where the journey of life would take them next.

Following the reception, they filled the Mercedes with wedding gifts—many wonderful things that would be useful in setting up a home in California. For their honeymoon, they drove the scenic route to California. Remembering his army friends, Siegfried thought, *I just wish they could discover the joy of living for Christ.*

Arriving in Loma Linda, they rented a small, furnished second floor apartment near the hospital. Evelyn accepted employment as charge nurse in a surgical unit. Later she transferred to the emergency room and also served as an instructor in the School of Nursing.

Siegfried struggled to find work. For two years, he'd been told exactly what to do from morning to night. He knew that if he went back to tailoring, he'd be punching time cards with a supervisor telling him what to do all day long.

Anxious to take initiative for his own life, he decided to go back to rock lathing. He contacted contractors he'd worked for before being drafted. Soon he had more work than he could handle even by working from dawn to dusk. To speed things up, he used stilts to nail up ceilings. Using stud jacks outside avoided wasting time setting up scaffolding and produced more income by the end of the day.

In summer he worked in heat up to 115 degrees. His hands were often numb from freezing cold on frosty winter mornings. "Whatever your hand finds to do, do *it* with your might" (Ecclesiastes 9:10). He was determined to keep doing his best.

Within a year, they paid off Evelyn's school loan and bought a new washing machine. "Why are we paying rent?" they asked. They wondered if they should go after their dream home or invest in an apartment property to increase their financial security.

They ultimately purchased a double lot on Stewart Street in Loma Linda. There was room for a modest home plus space to build nine apartments in the future. Both worked long hours. The first thing paid out of every paycheck was tithe and offering. Next came maximum payments on their property. Through joint effort, they were debt free and owned their own home plus an empty lot after only four years of marriage.

Encouraged by friends, Siegfried registered at La Sierra College to continue his education. With no special major in mind, he signed up for all the basic courses. He barely passed English—and a D in U. S. History discouraged him more. He got a C in Biology and a B in Principles of Religion. When anyone asked how school was going, he said, "They haven't kicked me out yet." *I don't have the brains to study, and I hate American multiple-choice tests.*

By the end of the school year, he accumulated 23 semester hours with a grade point average of only 2.23. He told Evelyn, "You can see I'm not made for school. I'm going back to rock lathing where I can make money and do something practical."

But there were many bright spots during the difficult year at college. Siegfried and mountain climber Hulda Crooks were sworn in as U. S. citizens on the same day. Even more important, he and Evelyn were blessed with their first child, baby Eileen. Hating to leave her with a baby sitter, he began taking her on his jobs. He put baby blankets in the bathtub and put her down to rest where she wouldn't be disturbed. People in the building industry began to refer to him as the only rock lather who drove a Mercedes Benz, did baby sitting on the job, and walked around on stilts.

In order to keep up with builder's demands, Evelyn often worked all day at the hospital and helped Siegfried at night. When labor unions tried to prevent material deliveries, he got around that by having the lathing materials delivered after normal working hours.

Siegfried accepted the position of deacon at the Loma Linda University Church, and Evelyn worked in the Children's Sabbath School Division. They also both helped in other church-related activities. At a youth meeting, Siegfried learned a song, "Make Me a Blessing."

The words of this song troubled his conscience. *What if Jesus asks, "Siegfried, what are you doing here?" My only answer would be, "Making money." I immigrated to the United States nine years ago. My first goal—freedom. Next, to improve my economic situation. These goals are realized, but isn't there more? Evelyn and I have well-paying jobs. We own our home. We drive a Mercedes Benz.*

He made a new decision. *From now on, I'm going to do something for the Lord every day.* At every opportunity, he began talking with people about spiritual things. He prayed, "Make me a blessing to someone, today."

Driving along Loma Linda's Prospect Street one afternoon, the Neuendorff's met Violet Riley, a telephone operator for the old hospital. "I have folks visiting me that you've got to meet," she exclaimed. At Violet's home, they were introduced to Pastor Marvin and Waloma Fehrenbach.

"We've just been assigned to work for the Campa Indians at the Nevati Mission Station east of the Andes in the Upper Amazon Jungle of Peru," Pastor Fehrenbach explained. "We're looking for volunteers to go with us, and we'd like to show you a film called *Savage Fire*."

Evelyn snuggled close to Siegfried as they watched a canoe capsize in a river full of crocodiles. A witch doctor ordered two smalls girls killed to appease the spirits. They cringed when savage fire patients screamed while being treated for a painful skin disease. They also laughed at playful monkeys. Seeing natives with bows and arrows, they wondered about the safety of the jungle.

The film finished and Pastor Fehrenbach turned to the Neuendorffs. "We need a volunteer with construction experience to build a clinic and a school. We're looking for an experienced nurse. I can't offer you a salary, but would you come as volunteers?"

Evelyn nudged Siegfried, "This is what I've been praying for!"

"Yes, Pastor Fehrenbach," Siegfried answered. "We'll come. Instead of trying to do some little thing for the Lord each day, we'll work full time for Him!" One question bounced around in the back of Siegfried's mind. *What will they say when they learn I'm a college dropout?*

The Neuendorffs spent the next few evenings learning more about mission life as they helped Fehrenbachs pack. Too soon, they were telling Marvin and Waloma goodbye with a promise, "You can count on us. We plan to join you soon."

Alone with Evelyn, Siegfried asked, "How long shall we stay in the jungle?"

"Eileen is three," Evelyn said. " I think we can stay until she's eight." They prayed about it and decided to volunteer for five years. After that they would need to go home and earn money to educate their daughter. They would build the apartments they planned for the vacant lot in Loma Linda.

After announcing plans to leave in three months, Siegfried and Evelyn were shocked by the response of family and friends. "It's a sin to take a three-year-old to such a dangerous place." "You don't have a college degree. Why waste your time?" "You're foolish to throw away your lives just to help a few poor natives."

Siegfried would always speak up. "God led us to accept this challenge. He will take care of us."

"You'll have to give up your jobs. How are you going to support yourselves?" people asked.

"That's easy. We'll sell everything we have and rent our house. The rent money will give us enough to live on in the jungle since we will live very simply." But doubt jumped in Siegfried's mind. *Am I too optimistic?*

Papa's words hurt most. "You always make bad choices. You're foolish to work five years without pay." Only Mutti and the German pastor encouraged them to go ahead with their mission plans. Everybody else was negative. "We can't let them discourage us," Siegfried shared with Evelyn.

The big test came when they started selling all the things they'd accumulated. They realized it wasn't easy to part with all of their possessions. Siegfried stood admiring their Mercedes. *How can I let you go?* He recalled words of Jesus. "Whoever of you does not forsake all that he has cannot be My disciple" (Luke 14:33). He left the car he loved with his parents to sell.

After three months of preparation, they were ready for departure. Money from the sale of their household goods helped them purchase mosquito netting, lightweight clothing, plastic shoes for river travel, dehydrated foods, tools, and other basics not available in the jungle. Papa and Mutti agreed to be responsible for renting their home. The Loma Linda University Church bulletin announced their plans asking people to pray for the Neuendorff's mission of faith. Siegfried purchased the cheapest airline tickets available.

Chapter 7
We're Keeping Your Passports

After flying out of Los Angeles, the old DC-6 settled down on the runway for its first stop at Mazatlán in Mexico. Passengers were ordered to deplane. With a Spanish vocabulary limited to *sí, no, Señor, Señora, and mañana*, the Neuendorffs wondered what would happen next.

Checking through customs and immigration, Siegfried grabbed Evelyn. "They kept our passports! The travel agent told us never to let anyone keep our documents." A group of officers stood together in a heated discussion.

Eventually, an officer with a translator approached them. "Mr. Neuendorff. You've entered our country illegally. We're keeping your passports."

Trying to stay calm, Siegfried replied, "We did everything our travel agent told us to do. If there's a problem, fly us back to Los Angeles and we can start over."

"No way! We can't do that." Siegfried held tightly to little Eileen. *Will they put us in jail?*

Airline personnel soon joined with the officers as the discussion continued. They kept talking, and each passing moment left Siegfried and Evelyn with more anxiety. They prayed silently.

At last, an airline agent walked over to them. "We are going to put you up in a hotel tonight. You can continue your trip tomorrow, arriving in Lima on Saturday."

Oh no! Siegfried couldn't believe that one problem ballooned into another.

He turned to the agent. "We don't fly on Saturdays. It's our Sabbath, the day we go to church."

They were placed on the fourth floor of a lovely beach front hotel. "This is sure better than going to jail," Siegfried smiled at Evelyn. "Let's enjoy it." He still worried though. *I don't want to be flying on Sabbath.*

Arriving at the airport the next morning, they were given a new set of tickets, their passports were returned, and they were escorted to the plane. "We're putting you on an expensive jet flight," the agent said. "But it won't cost you a penny more. You'll arrive in Lima at 7:00 A.M. Friday."

"God is good!" Siegfried exclaimed as they helped Eileen buckle up between them. "We've just started our missionary venture and look what the Lord has done. We paid for a cheap piston flight, and now we're on a Boeing 707. Best of all, we don't have to travel on Sabbath."

Their jet taxied up to the Jorge Chavez Air Terminal in Lima right at 7:00 A.M. Friday. Clearing immigration and customs, they were suddenly surrounded by men grabbing for their luggage. Siegfried shouted, "No, no!" as the crowd pressed in.

He spun around as someone touched his shoulder. "Brother Neuendorff, I'm from the Inca Union Mission. I came to take you to our headquarters." They loaded their baggage and began speeding toward the mission offices in the Miraflores suburb of Lima. Cars swerved back and forth as drivers not only honked horns, but pounded the outside of their doors. Two drivers even settled an argument with a fist fight.

That weekend, they enjoyed a delightful Sabbath worship at the Miraflores Church and dinner with a missionary family. On Monday, though, it was time to prepare for their mission. So they began studying Spanish with Nercida de Ruíz, a very dignified Peruvian woman.

But like college, studying Spanish was a difficult task for Siegfried. "It's a lot tougher than I imagined. My German tongue just doesn't want to twist the right way!" He became terribly frustrated studying all day and unable to pronounce the words correctly when tested by the instructor. Siegfried felt like a young colt wanting to run. *How much longer do I have to study Spanish?*

After one class, they took a walk enjoying the scenery and the crowds. People shouted *gringos* [foreigners] as they walked by.

Soon ready to go home, however, they suddenly realized they were lost. "Evelyn," Siegfried said, "I have no idea where we are!"

A taxi driver stopped by them, understanding that they were in trouble. As Siegfried tried to explain where the mission office was, the driver kept saying, *"No comprendo."*

Finally, Siegfried said, *"Adventista."*

The driver's face lit up. *"Si, si."* He then took them straight to the mission office.

⌒

Measles epidemics often wiped out entire tribal villages in the Upper Amazon Jungle. The mission president planned to go to the Nevati Mission Station with a load of vaccines for measles. "You are welcome to travel with me," he told the Neuendorffs.

At 4:30 A.M., they loaded all their belongings into a mission vehicle already filled with medical supplies. They drove out of Lima and immediately began climbing the Andes. In less than four hours, they reached Ticlio, the highest pass at nearly 16,000 feet.

Little Eileen became quiet and her lips turned purple. They soon realized she wasn't getting enough oxygen. "Just sit very still and breathe deeply. You're going to be all right," her mother encouraged. Even Evelyn began to feel strange. After an hour-and-a-half in the very high altitude, they started descending. Eileen began to talk again, and Evelyn also felt better.

The paved road climbing up the Andes turned into a narrow dirt road with one dangerous curve after another. Soon the bare Andes began to turn green and by mid-afternoon, they reached the jungle town of San Ramón in the foothills of the Andes. All their belongings, plus the precious vaccine, were loaded into a Cessna air taxi. The mission president climbed into the cockpit next to the pilot while the family squeezed into the rear seats and buckled up. Siegfried found the ride unsettling. *This is no Mercedes Benz.*

Lifting off the end of the runway, the tiny plane climbed out over an endless carpet of green. All signs of civilization soon vanished. *What will Nevati be like?* Siegfried could hardly wait to find out. *Will our lives be in danger? What will we eat? Will we be able to communicate the gospel to the people?*

The plane soon dropped to about 1,000 feet over the vast sea of green. Looking out, the family saw dozens of thatched roofed huts.

The mission president shouted, "It's Nevati!" The plane banked and turned to make its final approach over the Nazarateke River. It was breathtakingly beautiful. Below, they saw a huge sign formed of river rocks, "Welcome Neuendorffs."

They held their breath as the plane touched down on a narrow dirt runway next to rows of huts. Racing past Campa Indians dressed in *cushmas*, long robes woven by hand from wild cotton, the pilot brought the plane to a stop. Climbing out, they felt a blast of hot, humid air and began to perspire profusely.

Boys and girls from the mission school crowded around the plane with arms outstretched to shake their hands. They sang a song of welcome that overwhelmed the new missionaries with expressions of love.

The Fehrenbachs, Marvin, Waloma, and son Ricky, pushed through the crowd. "We're delighted to have you with us!" Pastor Fehrenbach announced. "Mosquitos will eat you alive if you stay in a thatched hut. We have the only home with screens on the windows. It's not ideal, but we'd like to share our living quarters with you."

"You are very kind," Siegfried exclaimed. "We don't want to be a burden, but we'll pay for our room and board." They unloaded the plane and with help of the Campas carried their belongings across the mission compound and up a flight of stairs to the mission house. The mission president gave instructions to his new workers, left the vaccine, and flew out in the same air taxi that brought them to Nevati.

Evelyn and a teenage Campa girl helped Waloma prepare a delicious supper. Waloma's homemade bread with peanut butter tasted marvelous. With the exception of bananas, the rest of the menu seemed strange. Papaya, a tropical fruit they'd never seen before, and boiled *yucca* [cassava], a stringy root that is the source of starch for tapioca.

Siegfried turned to Evelyn, "Looks like we will learn to enjoy many new things." Their diet changed completely. Meals consisted mainly of *yucca*, beans, corn, and sweet potatoes. Best of all—an abundance of fruit such as oranges, grapefruit, papaya, avocados, a never-ending variety of bananas, plus many other fruits with new flavors pleased their palates.

After supper and family worship, they headed for the outside shower downstairs. Only cold water sprayed from the nozzle, but the surprised Siegfried and Evelyn agreed, "We're missionaries now, so we will not complain." All water for the shower came from a galvanized roof that diverted the water into a 55-gallon drum. But there was one real blessing ... a real flush toilet.

Tired from a long day of travel, they went to bed early and fell asleep listening to strange new sounds of jungle insects, while dawn brought the songs of jungle birds making an alarm clock unnecessary. At 6:00 A.M., the church bell rang calling villagers to morning worship. Men, women, and children filled the church to sing, pray, and hear a Bible message by Pastor Fehrenbach.

After breakfast, they opened a jungle trading post where basic items like axes, machetes, pots and pans, flour, salt and sugar, noodles, cloth, thread, needles, mirrors, and combs were sold. Profit from sales paid mission schoolteacher's salaries.

Later in the week, a boy got a deep cut over his eye when he ran into a barbed-wire fence. "Evelyn," Waloma said, "You have emergency room experience. You do the suturing while I give the anesthesia." Siegfried held the boy's head while the nurses worked, but he fainted as he watched the blood gush from the wound, creating another problem for the nurses.

Each new day in the jungle brought excitement. Siegfried marveled when a Campa Indian used his bow and arrow to shoot a vampire bat. He watched in amazement when Marvin aimed his gun at a pit viper and shot this most poisonous snake right out of its hiding place in the palm leaf roof of the church.

Green parrots, brilliant colored macaws, monkeys, sloths, coatimundis, jungle cats, crocodiles, huge snakes and more lived around Nevati. Cockroaches were a pest, but the most troublesome of all were the tiny blood-sucking chiggers.

Wanting to be helpful, Siegfried accepted whatever task needed to be done. He repaired a stairway, dug a well, and helped with sales in the trading post. He also learned to vaccinate for measles.

To reach a dentist, anyone in Nevati would need to travel down river by dugout canoe to Puerto Bermudez and fly to San Ramón. No one could afford this, let alone have money to pay a dentist, so they often came to Pastor Fehrenbach seeking extractions. A Loma Linda dentist gave him a set of dental instruments and taught him how to apply anesthesia.

The first time Siegfried watched Marvin use a long needle, he felt light-headed and walked away before passing out. As days passed, he saw hundreds of extractions, always admiring the gentle way Marvin treated his patients. One day Marvin handed Siegfried a syringe loaded with Xylocaine. You must learn to give anesthesia," he said.

"No, not me!" Siegfried protested. "Don't you remember how I almost fainted the first time I watched you."

"The time has come," Marvin insisted. "First, let's pray with our patient. There are many things that can go wrong—allergic reactions to the anesthetic, a dry socket [no hemorrhage], or a dislocation of the jaw bone." He added, "Jesus spent a great deal of time relieving pain and suffering. We must follow His way of ministry."

Marvin guided Siegfried through the process. They waited for the anesthetic to take effect and Marvin removed a well-seated molar. The men began trading off. One would give the anesthetic and the other would do the extracting.

With Marvin's patient instruction, Siegfried began to do both jobs well. In one village, they were both extracting teeth. Patients commented, "These men are specialists." Words like that brought Siegfried the same joy he felt when he completed his first tailored suit.

One day at the close of worship, Marvin approached Siegfried, "You've been here for three months now. Tomorrow you will have the worship service." Siegfried blinked. *He's not asking me; he's telling me I will have worship. Doesn't he know I've never given a worship talk in my life! How can I do this when I know so little Spanish?* Accepting the challenge anyway, he started praying, "Dear Lord, I really need your help."

The Holy Spirit directed his mind to Ezekiel, chapter 33. He realized that many Campas living in Nevati are not far removed from savagery. They grow up trying to solve problems by shooting each other with bows and arrows. The spirit of revenge is law. Polygamy and the use of alcohol are major problems.

Siegfried wanted these folks to trust a loving God who says, "I have no pleasure in the death of the wicked, but that the wicked turn from his way and live." The verse continues with God's appeal: "Turn, turn from your evil way! For why will you die" (Ezekiel 33:11). "Lord," Siegfried prayed, "Help me be a faithful watchman and call people to repent from sin."

The next morning he stood with his translator, Juan Ucayali, who knew the terrible results of sin. He suffered as a child when his parents sold him into slavery by trading him for a shotgun. *I hope he will understand my poor Spanish.* He prayed again, "Lord, please help my translator make your message clear."

Speaking with a translator proved to be an advantage. Between each sentence, Siegfried had time to think what to say next. Relieved to finish his first talk in public, he thought, *While serving as a Hitler Youth, I would never have imagined doing this.*

Walking back to the house, he prayed silently, "Thank you, Lord, for impressing Mexican officials to return our passports so I could be here today and have this experience. Thank you for giving me words to speak. Thank you for always doing the impossible."

Chapter 8
Fisherman or Farmer?

S iegfried and Evelyn looked straight ahead—15 dugout canoes! They'd been asked to take a teacher to his new assignment up river at San Pablo. When the river became too shallow for the outboard motor, they'd climbed out and pushed the dugout.

Rounding a bend, they were shocked to see so many canoes. The river had been dammed off and Indians were dropping baskets of barbasco root into the water turning it milky white. Poison in the barbasco shrank gills, sending fishes to the surface gasping for air.

With fish popping up everywhere, men stood in their canoes shooting them with bows and arrows. Women and children standing in shallow water simply grabbed fish with their bare hands. The teacher explained that these people would be feasting on fish for days. "Fishing is our job, too," Siegfried said. "We came here to be fishers of men."

Siegfried and Evelyn returned to Nevati in time to join the Fehrenbachs in welcoming a group from mission headquarters in Lima who came to conduct an eight-day program focused on youth. Meetings all day long included devotionals, Bible messages, and health instruction. Campas were asked to build a campfire for the evening program.

Just as the moon popped over tall jungle trees, youths, their parents, little brothers and sisters, marched in and quietly sat on the ground. The meeting leaders looked in amazement at a teepee-shaped tower of logs that stood 20 feet high. They had expected a fire built with sticks not more than two or three feet long. Two youths lit the fire while folks sang:

Oh set the campfire burning,
Let's sit around the blaze
And store some right good memories up
To use in coming days.

Siegfried bristled when flames leaped up to 30 feet into the night sky. Joining others, he moved back away from the excessive heat. "I hate fires," he said. "It brings back horrible memories when I watched flames destroy buildings after bombing raids." He questioned why this was needed at all.

One leader explained, "We want the fire of the Holy Spirit to burn in the hearts of our youth. We want them to catch the vision of what they can accomplish when Christ takes control of their lives. We never dreamed the folks would build a fire like this. We'll make sure they have a small fire for the rest of our evening programs."

Siegfried continued, "For years I ran to bomb shelters for protection only to return and see new fires ignited by the bombings. For me, even a small fire brings visions of Berlin in flames."

"We understand, but please be patient with us," the youth leader pleaded.

The campfire story, *Clever Queen*, took place on the opposite side of the world in a jungle setting in Burma, much like the Amazon. The Campas related to the Clever Queen's experience in finding Christ. When a baby girl was born on the final night of the meetings, the young mother named her Clever Queen. Pastor Fehrenbach baptized many youth who chose to experience the fire of the Holy Spirit.

As work in Nevati grew, blocks were needed to build a new school. Siegfried took charge of manufacturing them, importing cement by shipping it up river from Pucallpa or flying it in from San Ramón. It all proved extremely expensive, so they used as little a possible. A Cinva Ram block machine helped solve the problem. The mixture—one part cement to nine parts of dirt.

A very long handle on the machine, invented by a Colombian, placed the mix under 3,000 pounds pressure per square inch.

Lifting the handle ejected the newly formed block ready to place in the sun to dry. During the Cuban missile crisis, Siegfried learned to lay block while building a fallout shelter in their backyard at Loma Linda. Having spent much of his boyhood in bomb shelters, he wanted to be sure his family were protected in the event cold war tensions provoked an atomic attack. Now he would use his bricklaying skills for God's work.

Laying block under a hot tropical sun took determination. Frequent heavy rain, at times lasting only minutes, but occasionally lasting for days made progress slow. Yet by working long hours, he completed the new school in record time. He also built a clinic. The Campas, who only knew how to work with thatch, considered the buildings a marvel.

After a year at Nevati, the Neuendorffs were invited to attend a ministerial retreat at the Inca Union College near Lima. Charles Case, President of the Upper Amazon Mission, visited with them. "God is blessing your work in Nevati," he smiled. Looking at Siegfried, he added, "Our mission committee voted to ask you to serve as director of our Unini Mission Station."

Siegfried listened in disbelief. *I have no theological training.* Thoughts of doubt raced through his mind. *How can I prepare people for baptism?*

Pastor Case continued. "Since you haven't completed college, I'm unable to invite you to serve as an overseas worker, but the mission will hire you as a national worker and pay you a local salary. Will you be willing to go to Unini under these conditions?"

Siegfried looked at Evelyn. Tears flooded her eyes. Mist formed in his own eyes as he reached out and squeezed his wife's hand. *I have a great wife. She gave up a well-paying job to be a volunteer in the jungle. I pray every day, "Lord, make me a blessing to someone." Praise God! He's leading our lives.*

Together, Siegfried and Evelyn accepted the invitation. Overcome by emotion for the opportunity to be official national workers, they knelt with Pastor Case, praying for God's guidance in the unknown challenges that would be theirs as they moved deeper into the jungle and further from civilization.

Returning to Nevati, Siegfried imagined his family would move immediately. One evening a shortwave radio message from the mission advised: "You will be replacing Israel Alomía at Unini."

He needs time to prepare for his move. Keep working where you are, but be prepared to leave for your new assignment on short notice." *This sounds like a military order. God must have been preparing me to be a soldier for Christ when he allowed me to serve as a Hitler Youth and in the U. S. Army.*

Time passed—a week, more weeks, a month, two months—and the Neuendorffs continued helping at Nevati. Shortly after dawn on March 6, 1964, the radio came alive. "A Helio Curier plane from the Wycliff Bible Institute is on its way to Nevati. The Neuendorff's need to get their belongings on the runway ready to fly to their new post in Unini."

The Mission asked Pastor Fehrenbach to accompany Siegfried on the first flight and present him to the church members in Unini. The Neuendorffs rushed to get everything out to the runway. Siegfried gazed at the sky. *God is so good. There's not a cloud. It's a perfect day to move.*

The plane touched down and rolled to a stop. Baggage filled all the space barely leaving room for the pilot, Pastor Fehrenbach, and Siegfried to squeeze in. Apprehensive thoughts filled his mind as the Helio Curier roared off the runway. *What will Unini be like? Will the people accept us? Will my family adjust to the isolation?*

Flying via Pucallpa, they headed south over the Ucayali, the longest tributary of the Amazon. An hour and forty minutes later they turned west up the Unini River. Siegfried sat up straight to get his first view of the Unini Mission Station located high on a bluff overlooking the river.

Below, dugout canoes hugged the riverbank, making their way slowly up river. Others sped along in the fast current flowing downstream. Beyond, the jungle rose slowly before suddenly forming the rugged mountains of the Gran Pajonal.

They landed on a short runway across the river from the mission station. Immediately they were surrounded by Campa and Piro Indians. Siegfried imagined that the languages would be very similar, but when he spoke a few words of Campa to a group of Piros, he discovered immediately that they were very different.

Pastor Fehrenbach introduced Siegfried to Pastor Alomia and the Indian believers. He suggested, "Just watch Pastor Alomia this first weekend and you will get an idea of the kind of program he's running." Marvin then flew back to Nevati with the pilot. Four hours later, the plane returned with Evelyn, Eileen, and the rest of their belongings.

It was Friday afternoon, so they rushed to get everything across the river and settled before the beginning of the Sabbath. Tired from the excitement of moving at a minute's notice, they went to bed soon after sundown worship. Siegfried fell asleep reviewing God's leading in his life.

⟋⟍

Like in Nevati, the native people met soon after sunrise for worship. The Neuendorffs thrilled to hear them sing. At Sabbath school, they watched the folks study God's Word. Everyone paid attention to Pastor Alomia's sermon. In the afternoon, they met again. The young people loved to repeat Bible verses.

Siegfried whispered to Evelyn, "This pastor really has the respect of the people. It's obvious they are getting good pastoral care." He worried at how the Indians would respond to him. *The pastor's been trained. What will I do with no formal training?*

Sunday morning Siegfried walked around with Pastor Alomía and noticed 15 head of cattle. "What are all the *Cebu* (cattle) doing across the river?" he asked.

"They belong to the mission. You'll have to take care of them."

"What?" Siegfried asked in shock. "You mean I have to be a cattle rancher too? What else does a missionary do?" Angry thoughts filled his mind. *I came here to be a mission director, not a rancher!*

A final surprise came just before the Alomías left. The pastor informed Siegfried, "I planted a rice field to give work to the church members. This will keep them from leaving the mission to work somewhere else. They need to have a little cash to meet their basic needs. I'm expecting you to buy this from me for what I've invested in the project."

Without realizing how much extra work would be involved, Siegfried agreed to pay the pastor and take on the project. Yet deep in his heart he was unhappy. *First he tells me I've got to be a cattle rancher, and now I'm forced to become a rice farmer. Why didn't the mission tell me all this?*

Siegfried worked to help the Alomías prepare for the move. Their household goods would never fit in a plane even if it made a dozen trips, so the Indians built a giant balsa raft and carefully loaded all the family's belongings, beds, books, furniture, along with 15 chickens and food for the trip. They built a shelter to protect the family from burning sun or pounding rain and a place to sleep at night.

Floating to Pucallpa would take five days and nights. Everyone in Unini came to see them off. Siegfried prayed, "Lord, please send your angels to protect the Alomías on their river journey. And please bless my family as we begin our work with these wonderful people." They untied the rope holding the huge raft next to the bank and the balsa drifted out into the swift current that would take the family to a much larger river, the Ucayali.

Siegfried stood by Evelyn watching the Alomías float out of sight. "The pastor is a very brave man. From the plane, I saw huge whirlpools. The river's full of submerged tree trunks and dangerous turns." Siegfried kept talking as they climbed the steep bank back to the mission house. "We're alone—just you and me and Eileen.

"No we're not alone; Jesus is with us," Evelyn reminded him.

"You're right. We need God more now than we ever have. I felt terribly lonely when I was sent to Hitler's Youth Camp in Poland. Fortunately my mother had taught me to pray, and I survived a very difficult year. God kept me then. He will keep us now."

At family worship that evening, they rededicated their lives to God's service. "Please, Lord, give us faith and give us courage. Help us to make wise decisions. Guide us in sharing Jesus by what we say and the way we live. Make us true fishers of men."

The next morning, Siegfried spoke for worship at the church. He stood at the pulpit with a Campa translator on his left and a Piro translator on the right. *Two translators will take twice as long. With talks for morning and evening worship, a Sabbath school lesson and a sermon, I'll need to make the messages as clear and concise as possible.*

After breakfast, Siegfried walked through the village. A brother called, "My wife needs medical help. She has a terrible breast infection." The man took him into his hut to see his wife. *Now what am I going to do? I'm no doctor.* He remembered that back at

Loma Linda, he'd learned that hot and cold compresses followed by a charcoal poultice could be useful in cases of infection.

First, with help from the husband, he applied hot and cold. Next Siegfried took a few pieces of charcoal, ground them, and made a paste placing a poultice on the infected area. After treating the woman, Siegfried prayed. "We've done the best we know how, Lord. You are the Great Physician. Please heal this woman if it's Your will."

Another woman came saying, "My daughter has the same problem." The treatment was repeated and again Siegfried prayed, placing the young woman in God's care. He just finished praying with the second woman when two men shouted, "Come quick. A young bull just fell in the ditch. It will die."

Siegfried ran with the men. Working carefully, they managed to get the bull out of the ditch and back on its feet.

Two days later, the women felt much better, but the bull was dead. *What should I have done?* Siegfried pondered. *When I was six, I thought the first bombers flying over Berlin were cows. I haven't learned anything about cattle since.*

Other major medical problems he learned to deal with included snakebite, eye infections, colic attacks, ulcers, diarrhea, vomiting, and parasites. Fifteen-year-old Melita came with an aching lower molar. With no dental equipment to restore the tooth, the only way to relieve her pain was to extract the tooth. *Should I try this with my limited experience? The girl is in extreme pain, so I'll do my best.*

The anesthesia infiltrated well as curious crowds came close to watch. He took his forceps and lifted the tooth out without difficulty. Melita declared she had no pain at all. Siegfried determined that with the Lord's help, he would always use the same gentle touch demonstrated by Pastor Fehrenbach in Nevati.

Weeks later, Siegfried walked into the living room. The rice had been harvested and piled on the living room floor. *I knew I didn't want to get involved in this rice project*, he grumbled. *It still needs to be winnowed and sacked.* It took several days to complete the task.

At last, village men carried the sacks of rice down the steep path to the river loading them into a waiting canoe. Delighted to get the stuff out of the house, Siegfried planned to float to the mouth of the Unini River. With a full load, he turned the canoe sideways to the current. It struck a submerged rock and tipped to the side. Water gushed in soaking the entire load.

"Oh no!" Siegfried called. "We'll lose everything."

The brethren rushed in to help stabilize the canoe. The sacks of wet rice were hauled back up the narrow path to the mission. They opened each sack and spread the rice out to dry in the sun. It cost countless of hours of extra work, but it was finally taken down river and sold to the owner of a riverboat on the Ucayali.

After reimbursing himself for the money paid to Pastor Alomía, he divided the profits with the families who grew the rice. He promised Evelyn, "I'll never get involved in a rice project again. I just want to be a fisher of men."

Chapter 9
Don't Go There!

Half way through a sermon, Siegfried heard a tremendous explosion. No!—just a flash of lightening followed by a tremendous roar of thunder. Immediately, rain pelting the corrugated metal roof became deafening. The sermon stopped abruptly, but no one left. Torrential rain outside would soak them to the skin in seconds.

Siegfried lamented. *Even the elements are against me. I have no training in Bible study or sermon preparation, so I struggle to prepare a message to inspire human hearts and it gets stopped in the middle.* He didn't know if he would ever get used to living where the average yearly rainfall was over 200 inches.

The Unini River often rose 10 feet during a storm, and the nearby Ucayali would rise as much as 30 feet. The storm eventually calmed and Siegfried finished his sermon. He did have one blessing—his Spanish improved each time he spoke.

For many weeks, the Neuendorffs received no mail. Nothing from their parents, no letters from the mission—not even a paycheck. To make their lonely life more difficult, Siegfried developed an ugly fungus infection on his feet. Evelyn treated her husband, but nothing worked, not even Penicillin. In desperation they told the natives about the problem. Elisa, an Indian woman, applied a jungle herb concoction to his swollen feet.

The next morning, he checked his feet. "Evelyn, look at this," he called. "The wounds are drying up and the swelling's gone. We're here to teach these people, but I see there's much we can learn from them." Soon his feet were normal and he walked without pain.

School children had been on vacation when they arrived at Unini, but now it was time for classes to begin again. The government required a college-educated instructor to act as school director. Evelyn, the only qualified person in the area, was assigned the job.

They also needed a full-time teacher who spoke all three languages used in the village. Although no one had been trained as a teacher, one woman, Elsa Valles, could read, write, and speak Spanish, Campa, and Piro. When word got around that a teacher had been named, children began to register for classes.

"Nothing in life is free," Siegfried declared. "Parents need to learn that education is valuable, but it has a price tag." Those without cash to cover the registration fee and tuition could pay with bows and arrows, artifacts, animal skins, or clothing. Parents paid with whatever could be sold to jungle traders.

When the school was going well, Siegfried looked for other ways to improve life at Unini. He called the people together. "You've seen the water pipe running from a spring to the mission house. Why don't we put running water into every home in this village?"

"Yes, yes!" they agreed. "We won't have to carry water from the river any more." Families were given the opportunity of paying in cash or with products. In a short time, every home in the village had running water with one shower head and a faucet for all their other water needs.

As the members gained confidence in their new director, he began teaching them more principles of health and sanitation. "Why don't you stop spitting on the floor in the church?" he asked. "It's God's house, and we want to honor Him." The immediate response was, "We will stop." And they kept their promise.

Siegfried made another proposal: "Every home needs its own outhouse. By taking care of human waste properly, we can avoid many diseases that plague folks in the jungle." In a short time, every family built an outhouse following the plan provided.

Friday became a special day. In preparation for the Sabbath, the main plaza and all around the church was swept with homemade brooms. Folks developed pride in the appearance of their mission station. They asked visitors not to throw paper or banana peels on the ground. Families planted flowers in front of their huts.

Visitors began to comment that Unini was the cleanest and most attractive village in the entire area. To make it more visible from the air, they carried river rocks to a rise off the runway and used them to spell out in giant letters, "ADVENTISTAS UNINI."

While eating one day, Evelyn commented, "I'm really pleased about the way the school is going. Elsa is a natural-born teacher and the children respond to her instruction."

"Yes, God is blessing," Siegfried agreed. "But one thing worries me. I've killed the rice project, and I hate being a cattle rancher, but these people need a little cash income. We charge them tuition to send their children to school and they have other needs."

Evelyn questioned, "Isn't there someway they can earn money?"

"Well, I've been thinking. The jungle's full of wild rubber trees. Perhaps we could encourage them to harvest latex. It's a product that's in demand."

Evelyn laughed, "You mean you want to supervise a rubber plantation?"

"No, but Jesus helped meet human needs. We must help these people reach financial goals so they can support their own school and church."

With Evelyn's encouragement, Siegfried applied to the government's Ministry of Forestry. They gave him a license to work in 12,350 acres—nearly 20 square miles of virgin jungle surrounding the mission station. *This is wonderful. It's far more that we can ever work, but it will provide an opportunity for anyone who wants employment.*

He purchased special knives called *rasgettes* to cut away the bark and small metal cups or *tishelas* to catch the liquid latex. The brethren carried the latex milk to their homes. Siegfried provided acid to coagulate the liquid to a solid mass. Then it was rolled out like pizza dough into large sheets and hung up to dry. The rubber industry proved a success, bringing a steady income to the Unini believers who gave faithful tithe and offerings on all their earnings.

⌐⌐⌐⌐

In a very short time, they came to trust Siegfried's leadership and judgment. One day, he called the villagers together. "You know brethren," he said, "Most of you are Christians. You believe that Jesus forgives our sins and gives us grace to obey Him. You want a home in heaven.

"God is blessing you. Every home has running water. Our village is clean and neat. Many of you are earning money working in the latex industry. This is not enough. God wants us to share our faith with others. He wants us to reach other villages with the good news that Jesus is coming soon to take us to heaven."

Everyone agreed they needed to evangelize the surrounding areas, but no one volunteered. A week later, Siegfried spoke with Evelyn. "I've been telling our members we need to go and share the good news of the gospel with others. It hardly seems fair to ask them to do this unless I go and set an example."

"You're right, Siegfried."

The next day Siegfried, along with Rufino Valles, their Sabbath school director, walked through the jungle toward the mountains of the Gran Pajonal. They each carried a few belongings in a flour sack treated with latex to make it water proof. "How will we ever find anyone living in this dense jungle?" Siegfried asked.

"Just follow me," Rufino responded.

Using machetes to clear the way, occasionally they found a broken branch indicating someone had traveled through the same area. Other times they got lost and had to backtrack. By evening they had crossed the Chipani River 20 times. Each time it seemed more difficult. Now on the other side of the river they saw a native family. Rufino shouted in Campa, "Where's the best place to cross?"

Water in the narrow river was very swift. Though not a very modest way to make their first missionary contact, they removed their clothing and carefully made their way through the swift current, dressing again on the other side.

The typical primitive Indian lives in constant fear: fear of sickness; fear of death; fear of revenge from another tribe; fear of the spirits; fear of the witch doctor; fear of wild animals. Siegfried noticed that the family kept their distance. He smiled hoping they would realize he had not come to do them harm.

The only thing these poor people could call their own was the simple thatched roof over their head. They had a few chickens, a mangy dog, an aluminum kettle, a machete, and a couple of baskets. They lived, ate, and slept on the ground, stretching out on a palm leaf mat.

The women offered their visitors *yucca* roasted in hot coals. Hungry after hiking all day, the dry meal satisfied their hunger pangs. People from other homes in the area came to see the strangers. Siegfried and Rufino began singing gospel choruses. Some of the folks joined in. One man had even met pioneer missionary F.A. Stahl as a boy. When they sang a song he'd heard before, he exclaimed, "Sing it again! Sing it again!"

Campas believe in *Pahua* [the great father] and *Tasorensi* [spirit], but they have no idea of a Trinity or a personal God. Siegfried pulled out his Bible and introduced the Creator, *Pitomi Pahua* [the Son of God], the one who made us, made everything, gave us 10 rules to show us how to live. The one who died on the cross, went to heaven, and promised to come back and take us to His perfect home in heaven.

When Siegfried told the folks he was going to pray and talk to God, the man who had met Pastor Stahl years before poked his son saying, "Bow your head and close your eyes."

Siegfried thought, *How wonderful to see someone with little contact with Christianity show respect for the God of heaven.*

One woman there suffered with diarrhea. He gave her a medication that brought immediate relief. Siegfried and Rufino slept on the ground with the people. In spite of being extremely tired from hiking in the jungle and fording rivers, Siegfried kept waking up. Suddenly he sat up. *What's going on?* He suddenly realized that the ground was shaking, and it lasted nearly a minute. *This is the worst earthquake I've ever experienced.*

As they prepared to leave in the morning, the people urged, "Come back soon to teach us more about *Pahua*. We want to know more about Jesus."

Two weeks later, Siegfried felt impressed to go where no missionary had gone before. *Just because everyone says, "Don't go there," doesn't mean there are no people to reach with the gospel. I'll take two guides and go to the Gran Pajonal.*

Siegfried explained his plan to Evelyn and Eileen. "You'll need to keep things going—the school, our village store, medical emergencies, and most important—morning and evening worships" Telling his wife and daughter goodbye, he said, "Don't worry. I'll be back in three or four days."

He left, heading for the unknown, with two faithful guides. Peaks of the Gran Pajonal reached to over 7,000 feet, and the lowest passes were over 6,000 feet high. Hiroíto Moreau led the way, followed by Siegfried and finally Moisés Ramírez. The trio was climbing steep jungle terrain when Moisés shouted, "*Maranke!* [snake]." Siegfried stopped and stood at attention. Moisés distracted the reptile while Hiroíto cut a stick and with one deadly blow, hit the snake in the back of the neck. Later that day Moisés declared, "God is with you Brother Neuendorff. Twice I saw you step on a poisonous snake."

Siegfried mused, "God's promise is true. After saying, 'Preach the gospel to every creature,' Jesus added, 'They will take up serpents, … and it will by no means hurt them' "(Mark 16:15, 18).

Reaching a hut with several Campas present, they sang choruses and showed pictures of the life of Jesus. "We've never heard of a loving God before," folks said.

Off in the distance, they heard the sound of approaching rain. Mixed in they heard the slow steady beat of jungle drums. *Is this the sound of war or a celebration?* Siegfried wondered. Hoping to find shelter before the storm hit, they hurried toward the sound of the drums. Men and women were drinking and dancing. "We can't preach here," Siegfried told his guides. "They've been drinking *mazata* [a potent jungle brew made by fermenting yucca]. These intoxicated people won't understand the Bible message."

The rain stopped, and they started to leave. A native passed by and said, "The river has turned into a raging torrent. It will be impossible to cross." Siegfried turned to his guides in disappointment. "Guess we have no other choice. We better stay here." The effects of the alcohol eventually wore off by evening. After singing Christian songs, Moisés translated while Siegfried told the story of Jesus. Folks who had been dead drunk when they arrived now listened attentively to every word.

At bedtime, all three slept like the other men with their feet facing logs still burning near the center of the hut. Rain poured down most of the night. Siegfried wrapped his feet in his raincoat in an effort to stay warm. Trying to sleep on cold hard ground, he kept waking up. When a rooster crowed at 3:00 A.M., he thought, *I couldn't have a more miserable night.*

Dawn brought an end to the rain, and Siegfried led the folks in morning worship. As they left, the Campas handed them boiled yucca. Back on the trail, they soon crossed the river that had been a raging torrent the day before. After crossing the river several more times, the trail grew very steep. "This is like climbing a cliff," Siegfried complained. His guides smiled. "You'll get used to it."

It took both hands and feet to work their way upward. Siegfried thought, *No one told me we'd be rock climbing on this trip.* He felt his energy depleting rapidly and prayed that he would make it.

The two Campa guides kept climbing without complaint, and at the end of the second day they came to an abandoned shelter and decided to spend the night. Siegfried laid down on palm leaves cut by his guides. His mind wandered. *How wonderful it would be to have a real meal for supper and sleep on a soft bed.* Tired, he dosed off, but kept waking up through the night.

He found no comfortable position on the unforgiving hard ground. Waking up again, he looked toward the fire and saw a bear. *No! I'm hallucinating. There are no bears in the jungle. It must be a jaguar. Should I give it a kick and push it in the fire?*

He took a deep breath, placed two fingers in his mouth and whistled forcefully. His guides jumped up. The wild animal he thought he saw was only a boy who had joined them on the trail. He sat there removing slivers from his feet. Siegfried thought, *I'm sure thankful I didn't push him into the fire.*

Glad for dawn after a restless night, Siegfried and the men ate palm hearts, a tangerine, and yucca before going back on the trail. Before reaching the ridge, Siegfried, not his normal energetic self for lack of sleep, kept stopping to rest. After crossing the ridge they began the steep, slippery descent. Siegfried grabbed a tree to keep from falling. He suddenly felt a sharp burning pain penetrate his hand. His guides explained, "Watch what you take hold of in the jungle. The bark on many trees is covered with sharp spines that will leave you with stinging pain for hours."

That evening, they stayed with a family who gave them a place to sleep on a platform where they could stay dry. For supper they ate yucca and a very special treat—a little salt. The host handed Siegfried a *cushma* to use as a blanket to help him stay warmer during the cool night.

The next day they climbed another steep ridge and looked across the immense Pajonal Valley and the jungle village of Oventeni. They trudged on, slipping, sliding, and fording rivers. At one steep riverbank, a large tree bridged a 60-foot span. Hiroíto crossed first. When Siegfried hesitated, Moisés crossed like a professional tightrope walker.

Siegfried climbed up on the log and stood there, his legs trembling like gelatin. *What am I going to do? Thirty feet below is a rushing torrent. If I lose my balance, it's the end. No one can call for an ambulance. I'll be washed down river and they'll never find me.*

He looked across the long log as his guides waited on the other side. He bowed his head. "Lord, you know how tired I am. I need your help with this one. Please send your angels to help me keep my balance."

He took a step and hesitated. He took another step. *I've got to keep my eyes on the men on the other side. If I look down, I'll fall for sure.* Step after step—he gained more confidence. Half way across he determined, *I've got to keep going.* At last he leaped off the log grabbing his companions. "God really helped me, but I don't want to do this again!"

They reached the village of Oventeni at midday. He talked with his guides. "I don't know what to do. We've been on the trail for three and a half days. My wife is expecting us back now. The people here are filthy. Pigs and chickens are running everywhere. It's no place to stay."

From the ridge, they'd seen a short jungle runway. *If we could just get a flight out of here.* He hoped to find someone with a single-side band radio and make contact with Unini or Nevati, but he knew he was only daydreaming. At a small store, they bought two cans of condensed milk and some crackers.

"Let's go to Nevati," Siegfried suggested. "We can't spend Sabbath in this filthy place, and I can never cross that log again."

They headed out in the direction of Nevati. While crossing a grassy pampa, another Campa joined them. "I'll take you to my cousin's house where you can spend the night," he offered.

He walked so fast they had a difficulty keeping up. Crossing rugged terrain they climbed, descended, and were constantly slipping, sliding, and falling. At the top of a hill, the Campa pointed across the valley to his cousin's hut. He whistled loudly to let his relatives know they would arrive soon. They whistled back.

The sun fell below the horizon just as they reached the hut. A few chickens and a skinny dog were in the yard. A log smoldered on the fire. *Where are the people we saw from the ridge?* Siegfried wondered. Now no one—just strange silence.

They walked around shouting *"Aviro? Aviro?* [Is it you? Is it you?"—the typical Campa greeting.] No one answered. No sign of anyone. Then without warning, a noise behind them grabbed their attention.

Eight men carrying bows and arrows leaped out of trees and surrounded them. Siegfried's heart pounded as he looked into faces painted solid red. Silently he prayed, "Dear Lord, please help these people understand we did not come to hurt them. Keep them from harming us." Two feet taller than any of them, Siegfried smiled. *"Aviro? Aviro?"*

They responded, *"Nakave!* [It is I!]" The tension broke and they began talking with Hiroíto and Moisés in Campa. They brought palm leaves for their guests to sit on. The women came out of hiding and served them yucca. Siegfried eyed his Campa hosts—filthy. *They're the dirtiest people I've ever seen.* Lips of both men and women were pierced and many had empty gun shells or a piece of bone sticking through the hole.

After the simple meal, Siegfried and his companions started singing. "Hmm, hmm, *kametza!"* [Yes, yes, very good!]" the Indians grunted approval. Siegfried told a simple Bible story. Realizing that Campas retire early on dark nights without a moon, Siegfried prayed asking God to bless his new friends.

Laying down to sleep, only a palm leaf separated him from the hard ground. He couldn't help thinking, *When I was baptized, I would never have imagined spending Sabbath with Indians in a wild place like this. Yet God sent me here because the gospel is for "every nation, tribe, tongue, and people" (Revelation 14:12).*

In spite of being welcomed by men armed with bows and arrows, Siegfried felt safe. A verse he memorized years before flashed in his mind. *"You will keep him in perfect peace, whose mind is stayed on You, because he trusts in You" (Isaiah 26:3).*

Chapter 10
Is He Really Dead?

Back at Unini, Eileen prayed for her daddy during worship on Friday evening. Evelyn worried. *Siegfried promised to return in three or four days. I hope he's safe.*

In the morning, the people asked Evelyn about her husband. All she could say was, "I don't know."

They explained, "The Gran Pajonal is a wild place. Anyone who goes there and doesn't come back in two or three days can be considered dead." With an aching heart, Evelyn took her husband's place in Sabbath school and church the next Sabbath morning.

For Siegfried, it was a long, long night on cold hard ground. Sabbath morning they were served boiled yucca and cooked bananas roasted in the fire. When breakfast ended, the men left to go hunting and the women and children went to their garden plots.

Siegfried and his companions spent a quiet morning singing, praying, and studying God's Word. Their hosts did not return, so they ate a few soda crackers for lunch. In the afternoon, Siegfried walked to where he saw children digging in a garbage pile. *What are they looking for?* Soon he saw them picking up large fat worms, smacking their lips and swallowing them with delight.

He also saw a woman who hadn't gone to the fields with the others. She searched under a pile of banana stalks. Siegfried approached saying, "*Nomitakotena?* [May I help you?]" She looked up with a large worm between her fingers. *I don't think she needs my help.* He cringed and walked away, thinking how far the world had fallen in sin. *God provides so many good things to eat. How can these people eat worms like it's a dessert? I don't know why we stayed here, but God must have a plan.*

Late in the afternoon, folks began returning. The oldest man in the family introduced himself. "My name is Huánaco. I'm the Campa Chief for this entire area. If you will stay a few more days, I'll bring all my people to this place."

With Moisés translating, Siegfried explained, "We're on our way to Nevati."

The old chief responded, "I've heard about the Nevati Mission. They teach our tribes to read and write, to sing, and to pray. That's what I want for my people here."

Siegfried knowing Evelyn would worry when he didn't return said, "We must leave in the morning, but we want to help your people. We'll be back." At sundown they prayed, sang gospel songs, and shared another Bible story with people who'd never heard what Jesus wanted to do for them.

After another night with little sleep on the hard ground, Siegfried and his guides told Huánaco and his people goodbye, promising, "We will return." Tall pampa grass kept their pant legs wet, making them feel miserable. Three young men they met on the trail directed them to a path they said would take them to Nevati.

With aching feet, they reached a fair-sized stream. "Let's build a raft," Siegfried suggested. "A bad ride will be better than a good walk." He watched in amazement as his guides cut balsa trees, tied the logs together with jungle vines, and had the raft ready before sunset.

They stayed in an empty hut offered to them by a family living near the stream. They got up early after another night with little sleep. "Five nights and no rest," Siegfried fussed to his companions. "I'm sure glad we'll travel by raft today."

They purchased 10 small papayas and three different kinds of bananas from the family who shared the empty hut, and then the three men climbed on the raft with all the extra food. Moving out in the stream, Siegfried thought, *Luxury at last—floating on a raft is like cruising in a Mercedes.*

They only rounded a few curves in the river when a man on the riverbank warned, "Leave your balsa here. The rapids and rocks ahead will tear it to pieces." Grudgingly, they pulled the new raft up on the shore, picked up their belongings, and began walking again. The path proved practically invisible. Hiroíto and Moisés found it difficult to stay on the trail. One time they had to backtrack several hours. They were forced to climb several mountain ridges.

Because of an infected heel, Siegfried had left Unini wearing thongs. Each step became more painful as they walked through mud in wet underbrush. Slippery rocks forced him to take off the thongs making it even more difficult to walk. By evening all three were dirty and sweaty. Their mosquito nets were wet. Even Hiroíto's cushma was soaked.

They looked at each other. "We're in for a miserable night. Up until now, we've found some kind of shelter or stayed with a family. Tonight we're sleeping out in raw jungle. At least we have some food for supper." They each ate a piece of yucca, a papaya, and a small banana.

Trudging along the next morning, Siegfried kept hoping to reach a river and start floating again. They found a river, but no balsa wood to make a raft. The dangerous trail along the riverbank was almost impassable. Moisés killed another poisonous snake that coiled to strike at him.

By evening they reached a stream about 25 feet across. With an abundance of balsa trees, Hiroíto and Moisés quickly built another raft. A woman with three children invited the men to stay in a hut near hers. They sang gospel choruses hoping she would hear.

They needed food and the woman sold them a stem of bananas. At dawn they boarded their raft and prayed, "Dear Lord, please encourage our families who must be terribly concerned since we haven't returned. Protect us on our river journey today."

It's so wonderful to give my sore feet a rest, Siegfried thought as they floated downstream. Looking ahead, he saw a man with a bow and arrows standing in the underbrush next to the river. *Where did he come from? Why is he here so early in the morning?*

The mysterious man called out in Campa, "Where are you going?"

"We're on our way to Nevati," the guides called back.

"No! No! Impossible! Stop here!"

"Why?" they questioned.

The man explained. "There's a waterfall just ahead. It will kill you if you go over it."

"*Pasonke! Pasonke!*" [Thank you! Thank you!].

They pulled the balsa to the shore, but the man who warned them was gone. Siegfried wondered, *Did God send an angel dressed like a Campa?* Hearing the tremendous roar of the waterfall down river, he realized their lives had been saved in a very providential way. "Thank you, Lord," he breathed another prayer.

Studying the terrain carefully, the men realized they shouldn't be going down the river anyway. "We need to climb another mountain range," the guides declared. They took most of the food they were carrying and handed Siegfried the stem of bananas. "You carry this," they said.

Climbing with his flour sack filled with belongings and a stem of bananas, Siegfried soon tired. Totally drained, he laid the bananas down. Without saying a word, Hiroíto picked up the bananas. He was as tired as anyone else, but the law of the jungle is to never waste food because you don't know when you will get more.

By evening they reached another river. Rain began pouring as Siegfried built a fire to roast yucca while the men built another balsa. The rain stopped abruptly so they also built a *tambo* [shelter]. They took time to wash their clothes and dry them over the fire. In spite of wearing two undershirts, two sport shirts and a sweater, Siegfried spent another cold night.

In the morning, they loaded their belongings on the new balsa and began navigating the swift river. Going through terrible rapids, Hiroíto, in front, was soaked to the neck several times. It kept getting worse—he washed overboard and had to swim to catch up. After going down 15 rapids, they met two men who said, "Leave your raft here and take the trail to San Pablo."

"San Pablo!," Siegfried exclaimed. "That's one of the groups in the Nevati Mission Station."

Moisés said, "Kametza! [wonderful]. Let's take the trail."

Hiroíto and Siegfried asked, "What's worse, take the trail and climb more mountains and expose ourselves to poisonous snakes … or take a rough ride down river?"

They decided, two to one, to chance the river, but it didn't take long to wonder if they'd made the right choice. The river ahead dropped, forming a huge crest of swift water flowing between huge boulders. "We'll never make it," Siegfried shouted. Using all their energy they managed to pull to shore.

"Brother Neuendorff," Moisés said. "You walk ahead to where the river gets calm again." Below the torrent, Siegfried signaled to his companions. The raft shot between boulders and capsized. Moisés dove in saving the raft while Hiroíto swam to shore.

Late in the day now, Siegfried said, "The weather is clear so let's camp here on the beach." Extremely hungry, they devoured yucca and palm hearts leaving no food for the next morning.

They had lost elevation and for the first time since leaving Unini, and they stayed warm all night. With no food for breakfast, they started early the next morning. At each rapid, Moisés walked ahead trying to decide the best way to go. When the rapids were too bad, they insisted that Siegfried walk ahead. "We're losing too much time," Siegfried spoke in disgust. "We've wasted four hours going through only three rapids."

The guides disagreed, but when Siegfried kept insisting, they finally said, "OK, let's try it with all three." The raft picked up speed flying between rocks. They crashed into a huge boulder in the middle of the river nearly capsizing. "See, I told you," Moisés shouted.

All three clung to the raft, which hung up on the rock. Hiroíto lost his grip and washed down river barely missing huge boulders. A strong swimmer, he managed to reach the left side of the river.

The current grabbed the basket Siegfried carried with his Bible, diary, mosquito netting, and other small items. Instead of sinking like he expected, the basket danced along on top the waves until Hiroíto dove in and caught it. "Thank you, Lord," Siegfried prayed. "This is another miracle."

Siegfried threw his machete toward the shore. It didn't quite make it, but Hiroíto managed to retrieve it. Siegfried turned to Moisés. "I'm going in. When you come, be sure to swim to the left side so we are all together."

The torrent grabbed Siegfried. At first it proved impossible to make progress toward the shore. "Give me strength, Lord," he prayed, finally reaching the left side of the river not far from

Hiroíto. They walked back toward Moisés and the balsa. "Come!" they shouted across the roaring current, but Moisés had his own ideas. He tied himself to the balsa, cut off the log hung up on the rocks, and floated away ending up on the opposite side of the river.

They used hand signals indicating they would follow the river, and when Moisés got to a place where he could safely cross, he should join them. Soon his path led up a steep hill while theirs followed the riverbed. They kept whistling and shouting, but soon there was no response.

Siegfried and Hiroíto stopped to counsel. "What are we going to do? It's 3:00 in the afternoon. We're out of food and now we've lost Moisés." Hiroíto found a small palm tree and cut out the heart. This helped to calm the hunger pangs of the two starving men.

The river turned the wrong way, and they were forced to climb another mountain range. Reaching the ridge at sunset they found an abandoned hut. To satisfy their hunger, Hiroíto ate flower blossoms. Siegfried found a dry corncob meant for chickens. Trying to bite off hard kernels, he broke the corner of a front upper tooth.

"Let's sleep on the platform under the roof," Hiroíto suggested. "That will keep us away from wild animals."

Everything they had was wet. Siegfried said, "Lets cover ourselves with our wet mosquito netting and put palm leaves on top. It should work like a cold compress and keep us warm."

Totally wrong, he shook and shivered all night. Between the cold and the hard surface, he slept less than half an hour during the entire night. In the morning, Hiroíto found a cow horn. Hoping to attract Moisés, he filled his lungs and by blowing hard, he produced a sound that echoed down the valley. He did this many times, but no response.

Siegfried worried, *Am I responsible for Moisés losing his life in some dangerous place?* As the sun rose over the Gran Pajonal behind them, they looked west. From their position on the high ridge, they saw the entire valley where the Nevati Mission Station was located. A thin layer of mist covered the area.

Descending the ridge, the two met a family living in filth who quickly gave them boiled yucca. This gave them strength to press on. Later they met a man Siegfried knew from his days in Nevati.

He was harvesting latex. He took one look at the men. "You must be terribly hungry. Let me share my bananas." Siegfried and Hiroíto each devoured five bananas.

"Let me guide you to San Isabel," the man volunteered. "The jungle's so dense, you'll never find it on your own," he said. Sharp pains from the ulcer on Siegfried's foot as he walked barefoot made it necessary for Siegfried to rest about every 20 minutes and slowed progress.

The brethren at San Isabel remembered Siegfried and brought out an abundance of food. "We have bad news," they said. "There's no trail from here to Nevati." Quickly they added, "We have a brother here who will take you in his dugout canoe." Siegfried's tired face brightened as they loaded their belongings into the dugout and shoved off. *God is really good. I couldn't have walked much more.*

Siegfried helped paddle as the swift current carried them toward their destination. Two and a half hours later, they tied up on the mud bank at the Nevati Mission. Immediately they asked, "Has Moisés arrived?"

"No! No! We haven't seen him here."

Siegfried worried, *What will I do? He wanted to walk and I insisted we stay on the raft. What will his wife and children do if he doesn't return? Do I need to go back and look for him?*

⌒

A Campa family invited Hiroíto to stay with them, but Siegfried limped about a quarter of a mile to the mission house, climbed the stairs, and knocked. Waloma Fehrenbach opened the door and blinked. "Siegfried! Is that you? You look like a ghost."

"I'm Siegfried all right," he declared. "I know I look terrible. I haven't shaved since leaving Unini 11 days ago. I've just walked nearly 200 miles from Unini through the Gran Pajonal."

"The Gran Pajonal!" Waloma exclaimed. "I've heard they kill outsiders who try to go through there. It's one of the wildest places in the Upper Amazon. Everybody says, 'Don't go there.'"

Excited and extremely tired, Siegfried stuttered trying to tell Waloma what happened. He got all confused mixing English, Spanish, German, and Campa.

Waloma wondered, *What is going on? I've never seen him like this before. He looks like a pile of bones.*

She said, "Why don't you take a shower. You can borrow some of Marvin's clean clothes. After shaving and showering, he stepped on a scales. *No wonder Waloma hardly recognized me, I've lost 15 pounds!* Marvin's clean clothes hung loose on his emaciated body. He began thinking about Evelyn. "Waloma," he asked. Could we use your short wave radio to make contact with the mission? I told my wife I'd be back in three or four days. She probably thinks I'm dead. I want the mission president to authorize a flight to Unini."

Charles Case at mission headquarters authorized the flight saying, "I'll pray you find a plane to take you. It may be difficult." Pastor Fehrenbach returned from a mission trip, and Siegfried enjoyed a restful Sabbath with the family who invited him to Peru in the first place. Enjoying Waloma's good cooking seemed like heaven. She treated the ulcer on his foot relieving much of the pain.

The Fehrenbachs joined him in making it a day of prayer that Moisés would find his way safely to Nevati and that God would watch over Evelyn and Eileen who must be terribly concerned.

Two days later, Moisés walked into Nevati. Back at Unini Evelyn and Eileen prayed constantly for Siegfried's return. The Campas insisted that any one going to the Gran Pajonal who doesn't return after two or three days has been killed. They told of bodies they'd seen filled with arrows like pins in a pincushion. *It's been eleven days*, she realized. *I might as well face the truth. The Campas are right. My husband won't return.*

For nights she fell asleep struggling not to cry. Holding back tears, she prayed, "Dear Lord, Siegfried and I promised to serve You for five years in the Amazon Jungle. I want to keep that promise. Eileen and I will stay. Thank you for giving me courage to carry on."

This brave missionary wife determined with God's help to continue working for the people at Unini. Without communication from the outside, she could only believe what the Indians told her. Siegfried spent the next nine days trying to get a flight to Unini. Pilots for the Wycliffe Bible Translators said, "We want to help you, but there is no way we can fit it in our schedule. Trans-Peruana flight service always said, "Sorry, not today."

Finally, a wealthy cattle rancher living down river from Nevati who owned his own plane agreed to make the flight. Besides taking Siegfried and his guides, they loaded 400 pounds of supplies for their village store into the plane. Profits on the sales would help pay for the flight.

During the flight, the rancher shared information that would help Siegfried better take care of the cattle at Unini. In 40 minutes, they flew over the area that took 11 torturous days walking. Looking down at the rugged terrain with steep cliffs, rushing streams, and waterfalls, Siegfried thought, *It looks impossible for humans to go through this and survive. My guides had to be guided by God for us to ever make it.*

Suddenly below, they saw huge letters formed by rocks painted white—*ADVENTISTAS UNINI.* Folks at the mission heard the approaching plane and began crossing the Unini River in dugout canoes. The plane touched down on the dirt runway and rolled to a stop. Evelyn, Eileen, the guides families, all the folks from the village came running up. "Siegfried, what happened? You've been gone 21 days. Why did you stay away so long?"

At worship time that evening, Evelyn spoke quietly to her husband. "Siegfried, I kept praying for your safety, but the Campas and Piros insisted you would never come back alive. I had to make a decision. Should I stay here or return to California? God impressed me that Eileen and I should stay here and complete the five years we promised to give to God's work in the jungle. I'm so thankful God is making it possible for us to complete our five years together."

Siegfried hugged Evelyn. "I thank God for a brave missionary wife like you."

Siegfried with Mother, Lina, shortly before going to Hitler Youth Camp.

Berlin Airlift during the Russian Blockade (1949-50).

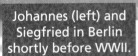

Johannes (left) and Siegfried in Berlin shortly before WWII.

Siegfried in civilian clothing while in the U.S. Army stationed in Hanau, Germany (1957).

Siegfried's birthplace, Karlweg 14, Berlin-Buckow, November 23, 1933—the same year Hitler came to power. The house, built by Siegfried's father, was the family home throughout World War II.

Siegfried, a former Hitler Youth, often hiked through the jungle to reach Indian tribes with the gospel.

Siegfried and Evelyn stand with Piro Indians at the end of the airstrip at the Unini Mission Station.

Siegfried uses a Cinva Ram machine to make blocks for a new school and clinic at the Nevati Mission Station. His wife Evelyn helps while daughter Eileen watches.

Siegfried stacking newly made blocks accompanied by Evelyn and Eileen. This was one of their first projects after going as volunteers to serve in Nevati.

Evelyn treats an injured hand in Unini. A few months after their arrival, their mission was served by a new mission plane, the *Fernando Stahl.*

Chief Huánaco (L) felt rewarded for all the work his people did when the mission plane arrived.

Mission plane, the *Fernando Stahl*, flying to Unini.

Pastor and mission pilot Robert Seamount baptizing a candidate prepared by Siegfried.

Siegfried and the Indians get a close up view of the mission plane with Pastor Robert Seamount.

Barry Black, first student missionary ever sent out from Oakwood College, spent a summer helping the Neuendorff in the Unini Mission Station. After graduating from Oakwood and Andrews University, Barry pastored seven churches in the Carolinas. He was invited by the General Conference to serve as an Adventist Chaplain in the United States Navy and became Commander Barry Black, Chief of Chaplains for the Navy.

Today Barry is Chaplain of the U.S. Senate, the first Afro-American and first Adventist to hold this position. He looks back on the time spent in Unini as a life-changing experience.

Barry carries gasoline up a steep trail to the mission station. On the right, Barry works with Siegfried as they prepare mortar for the new mission school at Unini.

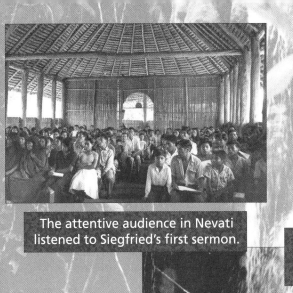

The attentive audience in Nevati listened to Siegfried's first sermon.

Juan Ucayali translated Siegfried's first sermon at the Nevati Mission Station.

Chief Huánaco at Tsioventeni. This Campa leader encouraged his people to cooperate with Siegfried in building an airstrip for mission planes to land.

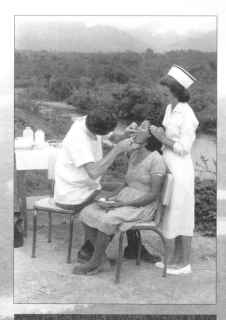

Rufino and Elsa Valles volunteered to be the first teachers at the new mission school for the primitive Campas in Tsioventeni.

Siegfried and Evelyn extracting a tooth at the Unini Mission Station located on the bank of the Unini River.

Sixteen-year-old Melita Diquez became the teacher at Tsioventeni after the Valleses moved to Pauti to start another new school.

Siegfried (right) travels by dugout canoe to establish new work on the rivers of the Upper Amazon. In the background is the Ucayali River, the longest tributary of the Amazon.

A Campa woman spinning thread from wild cotton at Tsioventeni.

A Piro Indian aims high at a bird.

Marivanchi at Tsioventeni with an empty gun shell protruding from her lower lip. This type of adornment disappeared when she accepted Christ.

Former witch doctor, Shawingo, and his wife, Marivanchi, turned from their pagan practices and became happy Christians along with many of the people from their village. Their faces are kind when compared with earlier pictures.

Siegfried (moderator) on
Channel 9 TV, Tacna Peru (1981).

Siegfried and Melchor Ferreyra television interview
in Tarma, Peru (1983). Pastor Ferreyra is currently
president of the Peruvian Union Mission.

Pharmacist Gabriela Vagas, Siegfried, and Pastor
Adan Mondragon, Channel 9 TV, Tacna, Peru (1982).

Chapter 11
Flight to Tsioventeni

A letter from the mission president urged workers to reach into new areas and build airstrips. "Our new mission plane, the *Fernado Stahl*, and pilot, Clyde Peters, will arrive soon to serve remote jungle areas. We want to start new work."

Siegfried announced to his family, "I'm going back to the Gran Pajonal. I promised a Campa Chief, Huánaco, that I'd come back. He wants a school in his area. Perhaps we can build an airstrip. Don't worry, my feet are well, and I have more experience. We'll have to ford many rivers, cut our way through wet underbrush, kill snakes, and we'll sleep on the ground, but God will be with us."

Two Campas, Rufino and Agustín, accompanied Siegfried as guides. While climbing a ridge to reach the Gran Pajonal, they became desperately thirsty. Agustín cut a jungle vine, held it over his mouth and let water drip in. Siegfried and Rufino followed his example. *These men's knowledge of jungle plants is amazing.*

Passing through Oventeni, they headed straight to Chief Huánaco's hut. The old Chief grunted, *"Kametza, kametza,"* when he saw Siegfried had kept his promise to return. While enjoying the chief's hospitality, they discovered he had several wives.

In the morning, Huánaco sent a young boy to accompany them to Tsioventeni, saying, "I will come later." The boy took Siegfried's bag and took off like he was on a marathon. It began to rain as Siegfried and his companions struggled to keep up.

Reaching Tsioventeni, they found both men and women with faces painted red, lower lips perforated, and an empty gun shell protruding through the hole. With or without the gun shell, saliva dripped through the hole and on their chin when they ate.

One village leader, Inkantiri, a young man with a positive attitude and a brilliant mind agreed to let the visitors conduct a meeting. Siegfried's prayer was the first these primitive people ever heard. He taught them to show reverence for God and His Word.

Siegfried took Inkantiri aside saying, "We want to help your people, but you will need to help yourselves too. You must stop chewing coca leaves, give up the use of tobacco, and refuse to use alcoholic beverages like *mazato*."

"All right," he agreed.

Looking around, Siegfried saw an old woman preparing to make mazato. "What are we going to do about this?" he asked.

"This is the last *mazato* that will ever be made while I'm in this village," Inkantiri assured.

Rufino spoke in Spanish to Siegfried. "My people need Jesus. I'd like to be a missionary here and share God's love and show them a better way of life."

"Wonderful!" Siegfried exclaimed. "Let's look for a place where you can build a house."

Soon Chief Huánaco arrived and they searched for a place to build an airstrip. The only possible site was on top of a ridge.

Since Sabbath would begin in another hour, Agustín, Rufino and Siegfried walked to a spring to bathe. Curious village children followed. When they saw the men washing with soap, they pulled off their *cushmas*. The men washed their bodies with soap. The youngsters squealed when they poured cold water over them to wash the soap away.

Back in the village, Siegfried conducted sundown worship with Rufino translating. The people learned to sing and listened attentively to Bible stories. On Sabbath morning, they conducted Sabbath school and church. These primitive people showed great respect as they learned about *Pahua*, the great God of heaven. The folks watched every move made by the six-foot, four-inch stranger visiting their village.

Sunday morning, villagers followed Siegfried to the site chosen for the new airstrip. More than 200 giant trees needed to be cut down with only a few axes and machetes. While clearing underbrush, a young woman barely missed being bitten by a snake hidden in sticks she picked up. Siegfried, not used to working with a machete, developed blisters.

After spending three exciting days with these new people, Siegfried and his guides prayed with them and encouraged them to keep working until they had a runway at least 900 feet long. Back at the mission station in Unini, the daily routine continued. Then one day, something wonderful happened.

A riverboat arrived with a very special shipment. A German family living in California heard about the needs for communication at Unini. They donated a small Lister Diesel Generator and a short wave radio that could operate on a fixed frequency.

After setting up the equipment, they were able to talk with mission headquarters. The mission president thanked Siegfried for the new work he was starting in the Gran Pajonal.

A few days later, the radio came to life. "This is Pucallpa calling Unini, Unini, do you copy? Over."

"Roger! This is Siegfried at Unini."

"This is Clyde Peters in Pucallpa. I hear you plan another trip to Tsioventeni. Would you like to fly? I can meet you in Unini tomorrow morning. It will save you four days walking."

"I'll be ready!" Siegfried shouted into the microphone.

Rufino Valles, a Campa with three grades completed in primary school, and his wife, Elsa, would make an ideal couple for Tsioventeni since they had no small children. He would teach reading, writing, arithmetic and religion. Elsa had already proven herself as a teacher in Unini.

The next morning, they took a few belongings and joined Siegfried on the Unini airstrip. The *Fernano Stahl* landed and taxied to the end of the runway. They quickly loaded their belongings and climbed in. Clyde asked Siegfried to pray. "Dear Lord, please bless our mission venture to prepare a new group of people for your coming kingdom. Give Clyde wisdom to fly us safely to Tsioventeni. Bless the people who wait to learn more about Jesus. Amen."

The *Fernando Stahl,* with its powerful 300 horsepower engine, lifted off and climbed to 8,000 feet to clear the highest ridges. Sitting in the co-pilot's seat, Siegfried turned to Clyde. "Since you've never been to Tsioventeni, how will you find it?"

"We'll go to Oventeni and then I'll ask you to point the way you walked."

Flying over the massive green carpet of jungle, it took 20 minutes to spot the 900-foot airstrip. The Indians had done precisely what was requested, yet circling several times the missionaries were shocked by what they saw below.

"Siegfried, do you see the huge trees at both ends of the runway," Clyde said. "I can never land there. The best I can do is drop you off at Oventeni so you can walk in. I'll come back in five days to pick you up."

Five minutes later, they were on the ground at Oventeni. They watched Clyde fly away toward Nevati. Siegfried, with Rufino and Elsa, spent seven hours walking through dense jungle to reach Tsioventeni.

They greeted the Campas saying, "Thank you for all the work you've done."

With Rufino serving as interpreter, the people asked, "Why didn't you land?"

"We wanted to," Siegfried assured them. "Before the plane can land, we have to cut down all the tall trees on both ends of the runway. We need to make it a little wider too. We brought three more axes and five machetes. The pilot promised to return in five days."

Men, women and children worked from dawn to dusk. To make it more difficult, they had to watch constantly for poisonous snakes. *It's an impossible task*, Siegfried thought. *The people are so energetic. I just don't want to see them disappointed again.*

Around noon, five days later, they heard the steady hum of the approaching *Fernando Stahl*. Clyde buzzed the new strip as Siegfried motioned frantically for the plane to land. He circled again and touched down. The soft damp ground made braking unnecessary.

Siegfried was shocked to see Waloma Fehrenbach climb out of the plane dressed in a nurse's uniform. "I brought measles vaccine," she said. "There's an epidemic in the Pachitea, and you know how this disease can wipe out an entire village."

Indians with bright red faces surrounded the plane. The men's hair reached their shoulders. Both men and women showed the tribal insignia—a perforated lower lip. Many had a 45-caliber shell protruding from the hole. They'd picked up the shells after hunters passed through their jungle area. Waloma had never seen people like this.

Clyde unloaded provisions for the teacher and his wife. "I'm sure glad you landed," Siegfried said. "As soon as you and Waloma finish the vaccinations, I want you to fly me to Unini."

Waloma spotted a fire. "What are they doing? Burning brush from the runway?"

"No, they're burning the brewery," Siegfried responded. "They promised not to make *mazato* any more if I'd bring them a teacher. They're burning the canoe-like vat used for making alcoholic drinks. Everyone used to sit around, chew *yuca*, spit it in the vat, add water, and then leave it to ferment."

"Then what?" Waloma asked.

"They'd have a *fiesta* and everyone got drunk."

Siegfried continued, "I'm amazed how fast the gospel changes these people. Our teacher's been here only a few days and the village is totally different from what I saw just a few weeks ago. They've even stopped eating wild pigs."

The tall missionary had no trouble persuading the people to let the nurse vaccinate them. She finished and Clyde said, "We need to get going. I'm glad Siegfried walked in without a lot of baggage. We don't need any extra weight."

They boarded the *Fernando Stahl* and Clyde prayed for a safe trip. "Wait," he said, "We've prayed, but I'm not comfortable with the soft strip. We're at 4,600 feet elevation. Most of the short runways where I take off are less than 1,000 feet above sea level"

"Does this mean I have to get out?" Siegfried asked.

"I think both of you better get out. Let me do a trial takeoff." The plane barely lifted over two stumps at the end of the short runway.

Clyde returned and organized everyone into stompers, rollers, and choppers. Women and children used bare feet or small logs to pack the soft earth. Men chopped out the remaining stumps.

After two hours, Clyde said, "I think we've done everything we can do today. I'll make another test flight. Perhaps the next time we can go together or at least I'll take Waloma and come back for Siegfried later."

Clyde returned after a second try. "We better take out some of the fuel." Attempting to lighten the plane, they siphoned out as much gasoline as possible. Clyde lifted off the dirt runway, circled, and returned shaking his head.

"You don't need to say it, Clyde." Waloma spoke. "I'm not getting in that plane. Let's find another solution."

Clyde affirmed, "The only solution is for you and Siegfried to walk to Oventeni."

Siegfried knew the trail well. "It'll take seven hours," he said. "It won't be a problem for me, but Waloma? Isn't there some other way to get her out of here?"

"The only way is to make the runway longer. The Indians have promised to do that, but it will take several days. Clyde, in the pilot's seat, leaned out the window. "I'll fly to Nevati and let Marvin know what happened. I'll see you about ten o'clock tomorrow morning at Oventeni."

Waloma watched the plane wave its wings and disappear on the way to tell her husband about the predicament. "Look at me," she mused. "I'm still in my uniform—and walk all night? I didn't even bring shoes. All I have are these thongs."

Siegfried laughed, "It's only been a few weeks since I walked out of here barefoot, and I thought I would die."

Waloma tried to borrow clothing from the teacher's wife, but everything was too small. She changed into a man's *cushma* loaned to her by Rufino and put her uniform in a plastic bag. Elsa gave them *yuca* and pineapple for the trip, they prayed, and the three, Siegfried, Waloma and a Campa named Juan, started down the trail.

The thought of going to Oventeni pierced Waloma's mind like a dagger. "That's where a commercial pilot found a body filled with arrows!"

"Don't worry," Siegfried spoke with confidence. "With our Campa guide, we won't have any problem. Perhaps we can spend the night at an Indian village."

In less than two hours, the sun dropped below the horizon. Juan stopped abruptly as they came to a jungle clearing. They heard the slow, steady beat of drums and wild shouts of dancing Indians. "Fiesta! Masato!," Juan muttered. "They make me drink. I no drink more. You go on. I go back."

"No, no!" Siegfried pleaded. "Please, stay with us! Isn't there a way for us to walk around the village?"

"No," Juan insisted. He dropped the bag he was carrying, stepped back into the jungle and disappeared.

"What shall we do now?" Siegfried sighed. "I'm glad Juan is determined not to drink, but I didn't think he would abandon us!"

"Let's keep going," Waloma said. "The Indians may be too drunk to even notice us. With the noise of their drums, they won't hear us."

Without a flashlight, she worried about stepping on a poisonous snake. They walked on in the darkness, sometimes stumbling and falling. "Angels have watched over us so far," Siegfried said as they walked on the dark trail beyond the village. The Lord will see us through the night."

After slipping in the mud and falling repeatedly, Waloma threw away her troublesome thongs. With bare feet, her toes pressed into the mud on the trail and she slipped less often.

At 10 A.M. the next day, they heard the *Fernando Stahl* fly over and land at Oventeni. "I wish we were there," Waloma exclaimed.

"Me too," Siegfried said. "We still have a lot of miles to go."

Hours later, with aching bones, a sore knee, and exhausted from a sleepless night, Waloma limped toward the Oventeni runway. Looking ahead at the *Fernando Stahl* and Clyde Peters, Waloma exclaimed, "This is the most beautiful sight I've seen."

Still limping, Waloma reached the plane. "Clyde, God has used you and the mission plane to save many lives. Now it's going to save mine." She backed into the plane and sat on the floor behind the seats.

Siegfried and Waloma had spent all night and half the next day to reach Oventeni. In minutes, flying with Clyde in the *Fernando Stahl*, they were back over Tsioventeni waving to people working on the runway.

During her short visit at Tsioventeni, Waloma called Clyde's attention to Marivanchi, wife of the village witch doctor, who had a terrible ulcerated fungus infection on her leg. Before he left Nevati, Waloma said, "Clyde, I think I have medication that can cure this woman's leg." She gave him the special ointment with instructions that Marivanchi be treated at the first opportunity.

On his next flight to the Gran Pajonal, Clyde took Siegfried's wife, Evelyn. Seven weeks had passed since armed Indians leaped out of the trees and surrounded Siegfried. Now Marivanchi showed complete trust in the missionary nurse as she cleaned the ugly oozing mess on her leg and applied the medication. She left a supply of the ointment with the teacher to continue treatment.

When Siegfried returned a few weeks later, Marivanchi sat on a log, pointing to her leg. "*Kametza!* [beautiful]" All of the infection gone, the skin on her leg was clear and smooth.

It's also *Kametza* when heathen people learn about Jesus and change the way they live. Missionaries marveled at the transformation in Tsioventeni. No one drank. The pagan-like ornaments disappeared. The gun shells came out of the lower lips. They washed the bright red paint from their faces. They stopped killing people with their bows and arrows.

About a year later, Marivanchi became one of the first from Tsioventeni to give her heart to Jesus and follow His example of baptism. Her husband, Shawingo, witch doctor for Tsioventeni, had used his bow and arrows to kill at least four people. He wanted to be baptized too, but chose to wait and make some things right first.

Chapter 12
Terminated

A t supper, Evelyn talked excitedly about how God transformed lives at Tsioventeni. Suddenly, she pointed to the wall. "What's God doing to us here in Unini? Look!: Big brown critters at least an inch-and-a-half long are crawling all over. Light from the kerosene lantern formed shadows causing hoards of invading cockroaches to look even bigger than they were.

The huge insects crawled across the kitchen sink and over the stove. They ran all over the table. Small red ants poured out from all the cracks and crannies chasing the invaders. To ward off their attackers, hundreds of cockroaches flew in every direction. "Let's get out of here!" Evelyn screamed. "The plagues of Egypt are falling!"

Fleeing their jungle home, Siegfried offered a silent prayer. "Lord, please stop the cockroach invasion." They ran to a villagers hut and were soon joined by several other families. Siegfried told the folks how God blessed the new work for Campas at Tsioventeni. Challenging them, he said, "It's time to reach out to the Piros who live further up the rivers. Many of you have relatives who need to hear gospel of Jesus."

Minutes before midnight, they walked in darkness back to the mission house. Evelyn reached for a flashlight that they'd left just inside the door. "Look!" she exclaimed, "The cockroaches are gone." Siegfried stared in amazement. "It's a miracle! God's promise is true—'I will rebuke the devourer for your sakes'" (Malachi 3:11 NKJV).

A few days later, Siegfried took three Piro Indians—Ulysses, Isaías, and Confesorio—up river in a borrowed canoe with an outboard motor. They prayed with every Piro family they could find. Anyone who could read was offered literature.

Hidden in the jungle, the Sepa Penal Colony, a maximum-security prison on the Urubamba River, housed some of Peru's most dangerous criminals. Men were flown in by DC-3 to serve life terms with no possibility of parole. Spotting a guard standing near a watchtower on the river, Siegfried cut the motor and shouted, "I want to speak with the head of the prison."

The guard yelled back, "Come and I'll take you to the Commander's office." Siegfried started the motor and moved the canoe to the riverbank. Confesorio watched the canoe while the other men followed the guard to the Commander's office. The officer looked at Siegfried and his companions with suspicion. "Who are you?" he demanded "Are you selling anything?"

"No, I'm a missionary. I'd like to speak with your men."

"You can't talk with prisoners today, but I'll let you speak with our personnel."

Siegfried followed the Commander to a meeting hall where 45 guards listened to a lecture on tactical gas warfare. The Commander stepped forward calling, "Attention!" The men stood like statues while the head of the prison spoke. "Good morning! Siegfried Neuendorff wants to talk with you about religion and the Bible. Everyone is to listen."

Siegfried had a captive audience. At the end of the presentation, several men expressed their desire to follow Jesus. One guard asked, "Do you have Bibles or Christian literature?"

"Yes," Siegfried responded. "Come to the canoe. I'll give you a Bible and literature too."

Siegfried and his Piro guides traveled on up river. On the return trip, Siegfried waved at folks on the riverbank at the prison intending to keep going. But something urged him to stop. He did a U-turn and headed back to the shore where a guard stood. "*Señor*, would it be possible for me to speak to the inmates."

"Why not? The prisoners are on break right now." He continued, "You gave me a Bible when I talked with you on your last visit. Thank you for coming back."

Siegfried looked into the hardened faces of thieves, murderers, and other criminals of the worst kind. For more than an hour, they listened to every word as Christ's love for sinners and His plan to save them was shared. A man who had taken 31 human lives said he felt a glimmer of hope as the gospel of Christ was shared.

Two guards asked serious questions about what they had heard. Then one said, "Jesus touched my life today. With His help, I'm determined to walk in His footsteps and keep all His commandments. From now on I will honor Jesus and His Sabbath regardless of what it costs."

Leaving the prison, Siegfried's companions said, "A borrowed canoe isn't practical for evangelism. We'll build a canoe for you." Stopping near Bufeo Pozo, they searched the rain forest looking for a mahogany tree large enough to build a sturdy canoe. Confesorio and Isaías, with only axes and a curved chisel, stayed behind to do the work while Siegfried and Ulysses returned to Unini.

With a growing membership, the little thatched church in Unini needed to be replaced. While waiting for the canoe to be built, Siegfried worked on plans. The men from the village helped him to prepare materials.

While working on this new project, he developed another jungle ulcer. When medications failed to bring healing, he remembered Jesus telling how dogs came and licked a beggar's sores. In desperation he let a dog lick his ulcerated leg. It felt wonderful, but the problem persisted.

Dr. Rippey came to Unini for a visit and found the ulcer crawling with maggots. He laughed, "The maggots will eat all the dead flesh and die." Not much consolation. The doctor left medication, but the wound still failed to heal.

Dr. Jeanne Andrews at the Loma Linda University Medical Center learned of the situation and sent antibiotics for staph infections. In two weeks, the wound completely healed. From then on the Neuendorff's used this medication to treat anyone with ulcers and it worked every time.

After waiting for weeks, Siegfried heard natives shouting, "Your canoe arrived!" He raced down the steep trail to the river. Carved from a single tree, the canoe measured 33 feet long. It could carry two tons, making it possible to bring in cement and other building materials for the new church. The stern had perfect dimensions to mount a newly purchased 20- horsepower Mercury Outboard motor.

Siegfried marveled. *How could they build this with only an ax and chisel?* He made many trips organizing new groups of believers on the Ucayali, Urubamba, Tambo, and Ene Rivers.

Evelyn and Eileen were home alone while Siegfried traveled up the Tambo River to start a new school at Bethel. While kneeling to pray one night, she felt something strange, soft, and smooth crawling over her leg. She looked to see a 10-inch tarantula!

Fearing it would bite, she froze. The huge insect moved slowly across her leg and disappeared under the bed. "Lord, help me," she prayed. "I'm not going to bed until it's hunted down and killed."

Campa Indians only counted to three—aparoni, apite, mahua. After that, it was simply more or many more. This made it difficult for them to know if they received the fair change when they made purchases. Piros counted to 1,000, making it easier for them to avoid being cheated. Both tribes discovered they were never short changed at the Mission Trading Post.

It's part of Campa culture not to steal or lie. Only once had a visitor started to walk away without paying for his purchase. Instead of accusing him of theft, Siegfried asked, "When will you pay for what you have in your *mochila* [knapsack]?" Without discussion, the man paid what he owed.

Peruvian laws guaranteed equal rights to all, yet jungle hacienda owners often flaunted the law in dealing with tribal people. A Campa male would often be required to work three months for a machete, a year for a shotgun, two years for a sewing machine.

As the work at Unini grew, more and more Indians learned to read and write. Large landowners on the Ucayali claimed they were losing control of their workers. Although illegal, primitive people were held as property and treated as slaves.

Fearing their wicked ways would be discovered, some landowners circulated rumors against the Unini Mission. The governor and judge in Atayala called for Siegfried to meet with them. After listening to Siegfried, they encouraged him to continue helping jungle tribes. The judge invited him to his home. "Will you pull a couple of teeth for me?" he requested.

"Sure, I have dental tools in my bag."

The judge sat down, and Siegfried said, "I always ask God for help before I extract teeth. Let me pray with you." A little while later, the judge, minus two teeth, thanked Siegfried and assured him, "From now on, you won't have problems with the local authorities." Many others came and asked for extractions too.

Traveling back to Unini in his dugout, Siegfried thought, "As a young tailor back in Berlin, I never dreamed I'd be extracting teeth. Thank God for giving me the skill to help suffering people and most of all for the privilege of leading many to Christ."

Near the end of the year, an invitation came for Siegfried to meet with the president of the Inca Union Mission. A kind man, Pastor Christman spoke softly. "We appreciate your work, but your employment with the Upper Amazon Mission is to be terminated on December 31. The committee voted to recommend you return to the United States to complete your education."

Siegfried's jaw dropped. A direct lightening strike would not make him feel worse. *Go home! I came for five years. The work is growing. We're in the middle of a church building project!* Words of a prophet popped into his head: "Why should the work cease while I leave?" (Nehemiah 6:3).

Siegfried took a deep breath. "What's wrong? Am I not doing my work well? Is there more you want me to do?" Thoughts of frustration tormented Siegfried. "Pastor Christman," he said, trying to gain composure. "I respect the committee's recommendation. We came to Peru on our own. If the Committee wants us to leave Unini, we will leave but we will not go home. We'll move to another village and work independently."

Even though officers of the world church body put pressure on Pastor Christman saying, "It's against church policy for a mission to hire overseas personnel on a national basis," he suggested, "Siegfried, why don't you ask the committee to reconsider its action to terminate your service?"

"Pastor, you can do that if you wish, but please remember we plan to stay in Peru."

A few days later, Don Christman met Siegfried on the street. "I've got news," he said. "The committee voted to rescind its action asking you to leave. We want you to continue working for the Lord in Unini. Insurance will solve the organizations' concern for liability."

"Wonderful!" Siegfried gave the Union President a big Peruvian *abrazo* [hug]. "God has answered my prayers again!"

He soon received credentials for the new year as a licensed minister. Mission officers ordained him as a local elder, making it possible for him officiate at communion services and call regular church business meetings. In addition, they asked him to serve as District Director for the Adventist Development and Relief Agency (ADRA).

Chapter 13
The Long Sharp Knife

T he dangerous Amahuaca tribe lived farther up the Urubamba River than Siegfried had ever been. *I feel reluctant to go there. Yet these people need the gospel too.*
During his first visit, he extracted 47 teeth in one afternoon. While extracting one patient's tooth, folks said, "A woman killed two children by holding them by the feet and slamming their heads against a pole until they were dead." Hearing this, Siegfried realized even more that these people needed Jesus.

That evening, he heard about an old woman who didn't eat and couldn't sleep. He felt uncomfortable as Amahuaca relatives led him in darkness along a lonely trail to her hut. *I'll just have to step out by faith and trust the Lord. Jesus promises, "I am with you always"* (Matthew 28:20). Entering the dimly lit hut, Siegfried stood horrified. A frail old woman lay on hard wooden slats. Only skin covered the bones of her naked body—her eyes sunk deep into their sockets. He asked for a sheet to cover her. Next, he said, "Please bring me a basin of warm water, soap, and a soft rag."

"Dear Lord," Siegfried prayed. "Please help this woman feel better." Slowly he began giving her a bed bath. Within minutes she closed her eyes and began breathing deeply. She had fallen asleep. Before leaving in the morning, he asked family members, "How's your mother doing? "

They replied, "She slept all night and ate this morning for the first time in many days."

"Thank you, Lord for another miracle," Siegfried prayed. "Your power and a simple water treatment has opened doors for us to reach another tribe."

One evening back in Unini, he heard a terrible commotion. People shouted, "A man's been murdered on the other side of the river." Siegfried grabbed a flashlight, hurried to his canoe, and crossed the river. The crime took place beyond the mission property.

Reaching the site, he looked in horror. An Indian lay on the ground, an arrow piercing his chest and his bloody skull split wide open. The victim had flirted with his neighbor's wife. In Campa fashion, the husband waited to avenge himself. At close range, he put an arrow through the man's chest. Then he used his bow to break the man's skull. With an aching heart, Siegfried prayed, "Lord, help me keep giving the gospel. Let the Holy Spirit change these people's lives."

With the new church at Unini completed, and with many new groups being formed along the rivers and in the Gran Pajonal, Siegfried invited everyone to come to Unini for a combination Camp Meeting, Youth Week of Prayer, and Junior Camp all in one.

Personnel from Lima arrived in the mission plane. Piros came in dugout canoes. Campas walked up a trail along the Unini River. Folks from Tsioventeni hiked three days through dense jungle. These precious people, led by former the witch doctor Shawingo, camped on the dirt floor of the old thatched church.

They rose before sunrise each morning for prayer bands. Shawingo asked the blessing on their food before each meal. Siegfried and Evelyn rejoiced to see people, who a short time before worshiped spirits, coming to worship the God of heaven. At the end of eight days, Shawingo, who had used his bow and arrow in the past to kill at least four men, was baptized along with many others. His wife, Marivanchi, had been baptized the year before by Pastor Robert Seamount.

Student missionaries often came and spent time with the Neuendorffs. Each one had special skills. They helped on construction projects, participated in church activities, and accompanied Siegfried on mission trips. Evelyn turned on the shortwave radio one evening. "This is Lima calling Unini, Lima calling Unini." She answered and called to Siegfried. "The Youth Director at Inca Union Mission headquarters wants to talk with you."

"Brother Neuendorff, student missionaries who've worked with you always come back with good reports. We have a letter from the General Conference asking if we would accept a student from Oakwood College. They've never sent out a black student before. Would you and Evelyn be willing to have a student from Oakwood spend a summer with you?"

Siegfried almost dropped his microphone. *How will jungle people react to an African American? At the Hitler Youth Camp, they constantly brainwashed us to believe Germans are a superior race. The German Reich put blacks at the bottom of the totem pole.*

Speaking into the microphone he said, "A black soldier pulled a knife on me when I was serving in the army. You want me to take a student from Oakwood?" He hesitated. "Of course, we'll be glad to have an African American student. That's what the gospel is all about. We're all brothers in Christ. Jesus died for everyone."

"Thank you, Siegfried! I knew you'd be willing," the voice in Lima responded. "We will keep you informed as it all works out."

In early June, a Boeing 707 touched down at Jorge Chavez International Airport in Lima. Barry Black, wearing a beard, rushed down the ramp and began asking questions: "Are there crocodiles? I'm really worried about jaguars. What about anopheles mosquitoes? I've had all kinds of shots, but nothing for malaria."

After evening worship at a missionary home, the pastor explained, "Several young Americans with beards have been arrested in the Peruvian jungle because the government believes anyone wearing a beard is sympathetic with Che Guevarra and communism. For your own safety, it will be best if you shave."

The young man, who grew up in the ghettos of Baltimore, didn't quite know what to make of this. "I don't have a razor," he said.

"No problem, I'll loan you mine," the pastor offered.

Minutes later, Barry came out of the bathroom—his beard gone. "Thank you Barry, for respecting our request. God will bless your service with the Neuendorff family. Right now, they're building a new church and holding evangelistic meetings in the jungle town of Bolognesi."

Fifteen hours after disembarking in Lima, Barry boarded a crowded bus that climbed to 15,806 feet in the Andes before descending around a thousand turns to where the Amazon Jungle begins. Minutes after reaching an airstrip in San Ramón, he squeezed into a tiny Super Cub.

The mission pilot prayed, and seconds later they were over deep green jungle. The flight ended when the plane dropped low over the Ucayali River and landed on Bolognesi's rough airstrip. Siegfried and Evelyn ran to the plane. "Welcome Barry! We're so glad you came."

Siegfried wondered, *How will this young man react to the challenges of mission life in the jungle?* He explained, "We've finished our work here for now. We need to leave soon in order to reach the Unini Mission Station before Sabbath.

The Neuendorffs and Barry carried their baggage to the canoe. Siegfried yanked the starter cord on the outboard engine and they began moving up the Ucayali. Barry watched as they passed dugouts floating down the river while colorful jungle birds flew overhead.

After rounding a few bends in the river, the sun lowered on the horizon. Siegfried spotted a sandy beach where they could spend the night. He smiled as they climbed out of the canoe. "Sometimes we chase crocodiles off the beaches where we sleep."

Barry saw animal tracks in the sand. *I'd better be prepared,* he worried. *I don't want to be supper for a jaguar or crocodile.* Siegfried cringed when he pulled a long sharp knife out of his baggage and placed it next to his sleeping bag. "Barry!" he called. "We live by faith in the mission field. Please put the knife away." Reluctantly, Barry complied.

Shortly after midnight, the stars disappeared and it began to rain. Not expecting rain in the dry season, they were unprepared—no plastic, no tarp, no way to stay dry. It was still dark when Siegfried called, "Time to rise and shine. We want to reach Unini before Sabbath."

Barry rolled over and crawled slowly out of his sleeping bag. The only dry spot on the beach was where his body touched the ground. He rolled up the wet sleeping bag, walked slowly to the river edge, and tossed it in the canoe. Standing next to the muddy river, he stretched out his arms and looked up. "Lord, if this is the beginning, what will the end be like?"

At Unini, Barry adjusted quickly to the difficulties of mission life. He was always ready to do whatever needed to be done. He and Siegfried worked together under the blazing Amazon sun, laying bricks to complete a new school. He learned to sing solos in Spanish and sang for meetings.

Dark skinned Indians often touched Barry's black skin, curious to see what it's like to have skin darker than theirs. While growing up in a Baltimore ghetto, Barry became a disciple of Malcom X and arrived in Unini with a chip on his shoulder. "Black is beautiful," he would say.

When he raised the subject of *black power*, Siegfried smiled, "I don't know what you're talking about. My interest is in the power of the Holy Spirit. Our job is to reach every tribe and tongue and people and help them be ready for heaven. We must answer Christ's prayer, 'That they may be one as we *are*'" (John 17:11). (Siegfried says the race topic never came up again. Barry declares Siegfried showed great deal of patience and love in putting up with his sometimes bitter spirit.)

Ever since opening up work in the Gran Pajonal, Siegfried made frequent visits to Tsioventeni, often walking. After sending Rufino and Elsa Valles to start a new school in Pauti, he recruited a 16-year-old girl to teach at Tsioventeni. Melita Diquez, a Campa Indian, with only a primary school education conducted morning and evening worships, taught school, and preached Sabbath sermons. Her leadership helped settle many conflicts in the village.

Siegfried, anxious to see how the work of the Valles family progressed at Pauti, arranged for the mission plane to fly him and Barry to the remote village. Pilot Clyde Peters promised to pick them up after five days. When he didn't return, Siegfried figured the plane must be down for repairs or some other problem.

"Barry," he said, "I have appointments to meet. We'll have to walk to Oventeni."

Barry accepted the challenge, but soon discovered he needed the energy of an Olympic athlete to keep up with Siegfried. Before long they were jumping over fallen trees, stumbling on rocks, wading rivers, crawling and slipping. In one place, they could easily have lost their lives by falling several hundred feet over a precipice.

"Brother Neuendorff," Barry said, "If you'd told me it would be like this, I would have refused to come. I'd be back in Pauti waiting for the mission plane!"

Exhausted after eight hours walking to reach Oventeni, Barry reflected, *A jungle hike like we had today builds tremendous faith that Christ will see you through. It makes one totally dependent on God.*

They were getting ready to pray together when they heard the sound of an airplane. Clyde Peters landed in the Mission's Super Cub. With the engine still running he shouted, "The sun's almost down. Get in the plane now or stay here for the weekend." They ran and climbed in the tiny plane. Twenty minutes flying put them back in Unini. It would have taken three days to walk. Barry thought, *The airplane is a great tool for evangelism in a jungle setting like this.*

He began referring to trips on the river with Siegfried as *canoeing for Christ.* Each time they passed the Sepa Prison, they stopped to hold meetings and give Bible studies. Barry helped Siegfried extract teeth in many Indian villages.

One evening they stopped at a small settlement. Several families came out. Barry stood in the bow of the canoe and sang, "Lord, I'm Coming Home." The last rays of sun touched his face as he finished singing. One man on the bank, moved by Barry's song stepped forward saying, "My family and I want to be baptized right now."

Siegfried explained, we want you to be baptized, but first you need to study and learn what serving Jesus is all about. He arranged for a layman to give the folks Bible studies. Several months later, this family and several others were baptized.

On the way to the Lima airport for his flight home, Barry said, "When I came to Peru, my chief interests were politics and philosophy. After three months with Siegfried, I'm interested in the Bible and the Spirit of Prophecy."

His last words before boarding the plane back to the states were these: "Whether it's among the ghetto people in the asphalt jungles of our American cities or among primitive tribes of the world's most remote areas, I know my real joy will be in serving others."

The love Barry Black received while living and working in the jungle with the Neuendorff's melted his heart. He returned to Oakwood and switched to a theology major. He never forgot—our safety comes from trust in God, not a knife. Back in the states, when sharing his experience with Siegfried, he said, "I saw Christ in this man. He treated me like a son."

Chapter 14
Who Do You Think You Are?

Cristóbal Corrales [not his real name] came to Sepa Prison to complete a life sentence for murdering 31 people. In a fit of anger, he killed the prison baker, cut his body in pieces, and shoved them into the large prison oven. Yet conviction grew in this wicked man's heart after hearing about the amazing love of Jesus during one of Siegfried's first visits.

While taking Bible studies, Cristóbal discovered that "the blood of Jesus Christ His Son cleanses us from all sin" (1 John 1:7). God can forgive a man who took 32 human lives. Prison officials, seeing the unbelievable transformation in one of their worst prisoners, permitted a visiting pastor to baptize Cristóbal in the Ucayali. This murderer came up out of the muddy river determined to be a faithful witness to his fellow prisoners.

Siegfried built two clinics, two schools, and two churches. With Evelyn's supervision, they operated six schools—Unini, Tsioventeni, Pauti, Tambo, Betani, and Bethel. He extracted over 6,000 teeth. Ninety new people were baptized—people like Cristóbal, Marivanchi, Shawingo, and even Chief Huánaco's son.

General Conference President Robert Pierson visited Unini and marveled at the order and cleanliness of the village. He watched tribal people enter the church to worship and pray. He saw children of former uneducated natives doing excellent work in school. He witnessed the loving attention that Siegfried and Evelyn gave to the needs of Campas and Piros.

Before leaving, he put his hand on Siegfried's shoulder. "Brother Neuendorff, the Lord has blessed you and your wife. We appreciate your work. Why don't you study to become a pastor? We'd love to have you serve as a regular full-time overseas missionaries."

Evelyn and Eileen were standing there too. "Let's pray together?" Pastor Pierson suggested. "Dear Lord, we thank you for the sacrifice the Neuendorffs have made to give the gospel to people here in the jungle. Please guide them in all their future plans."

No one said, "You've got to do this." Siegfried and Evelyn talked it over without feeling pressure. "It does seem this kind church leader wants the best for our future. We came for five years, and we've been here six. Let's accept the counsel from the head of our world church."

The next time the mission plane came, Siegfried sent his letter of resignation to the Upper Amazon Mission. Almost immediately, Pastor Andrés Achata contacted him by radio. "We don't want you to leave."

"Pastor Achata," Siegfried responded, "Our decision is made. We're not getting younger. If I'm ever going to study, I must do it now."

"All right, if you insist, I'll share this with our mission committee and ask them to recommend to the Union that your plans be approved. You'll get a letter of appreciation for all the work you've done."

"Be assured Pastor," Siegfried said, "This is not an easy decision. We'll miss the precious people we've shared the gospel with, the beauty of the lush green jungle, and the majestic mountains I've walked over so many times. Most of all we'll miss seeing people learn about Jesus for the first time. Yes, we are leaving, but our hearts will stay."

D.J. Sandstrom, President of the Inca Union wrote: "We approved your request to return to the United States. No one wants you to leave, but all understand your desire to study for the ministry. It's our wish to have you return when you complete your studies."

Purchasing tickets to the States wiped out the couple's savings. Renters vacated so they could live in their own home, but they desperately needed money. Evelyn got a job in the cardiac unit at the Loma Linda University Medical Center. Siegfried prayed, "Lord, help me to find work too."

Reflecting on his service as a medic in the U. S. Army, he applied for work as an orderly before summer school began. "You're hired," he was told after filling out a form. "Thank you, Lord, for answering my prayer so quickly." The staffing nurse took him to his office on the second floor. *Office?* Siegfried gulped. No desk, no phone—only a high bed, a shower, and a toilet. *What will I be doing here?* He didn't have to wait long to find out.

"Mr. Neuendorff, you will be the prep-orderly for all men having surgery in this hospital."

"What does that mean? What will I have to do?"

"You will shave the patients and give them an enema followed by a Phisohex shower."

Stunned, Siegfried looked at the floor. *Am I hearing correctly? Give enemas? As a mission director, I initiated toilet construction, but I've never done anything like this.*

Siegfried dressed in white slacks, a white shirt, and a black bow tie, and wore a pager. Each time he was called, he responded, "University Prep-Orderly, how may I help you?" He playfully added *university* to make his job sound more dignified.

Soon he realized he was actually the last person to communicate with the patients before they took their pre-op medication. *Men come from all kinds of backgrounds and many are afraid. At least I can show concern and love for each one.*

One patient, a short, stocky middle-aged man with a well-built body entered the office. "Young man, I'm a prizefighter. If you cut me, I'll punch you right through the door!" Siegfried made sure the door wasn't locked in case he needed to escape quickly.

After surgery, the prizefighter thanked him for excellent service. Another patient noticed his name tag. "Neuendorff! You speak with an accent. Are you from Germany? "

"Yes, I'm from Berlin."

The patient paused, "Do you remember the night of November 22, 1943?"

"I surely do! November 23 is my birthday, and we had a terrible bomb attack the night before."

"You know what!" the patient explained. "I was up above in a B-17 bomber pulling the trigger and you were below."

Leaning over to finish shaving his patient, Siegfried said, "Sir, that was then. Now I'm above and you're below." Both men had a good laugh.

Still working as a prep-orderly, Siegfried registered for summer school at Loma Linda University's La Sierra Campus. After living out of the states for so long, he found himself frightened when taking a simple test to renew his driver's license. He passed, but how well would he do on college exams? *I didn't do well when I tried college before.*

Another concern—*Should I major in religion or theology?* He prayed for guidance. The next day, he met Pastor Robert Pierson in front of the hospital. "During your visit to the Unini Mission Station, you counseled me to study. Should I major in religion or theology?"

The church leader responded, "Take the shortest course possible so you can get back to the mission field.

"And pastor, what if the General Conference doesn't call me when I finish?"

"If that happens, just contact me."

Siegfried thought it over. *The shortest course is religion, and it will keep me from taking Greek. But if I ever want to minister in the United States, they'll want me to have a degree in theology.* He chose theology even though he considered Greek a terrible threat. His decision made, he thanked the Lord for leading. *With God's help I will complete my education.*

Enrolling in summer school, he took Dr. Norval Pease's class in New Testament Epistles. He enjoyed learning more of God's amazing grace from Paul, Peter, and John, but received a C- on his first test. *Oh, no! I've studied every possible moment. If I'm doing this bad in a class I love, what will happen when I take Greek?*

During the fall semester, Siegfried took several more classes from Dr. Pease. After getting several A's, Dr. Pease said, "You know Siegfried, I had you classified as a C student. God is helping you learn how to study and then put what you learned on the test sheet."

Siegfried thanked the Lord when Dr. Madelyn Haldeman gave him an A in Greek. Other required classes were Philosophy, Gregorian Chants, and Shakespeare. *What good will this stuff do me in the mission field?*

Ten years older than most of his classmates, Siegfried felt sad when many dropped out. He tried to encourage every one he could. "You young men have been studying all your lives. I've been in the school of hard knocks and learned the practical side of life. Don't give up! All this theory and book learning can't be compared with the joy of serving as a pastor and winning people for Christ."

Evelyn watched her husband struggle to reach his goals. "Siegfried," she said, "Why don't you quit your job at the hospital. There's no sense killing yourself. I think we can live on my salary and still pay your tuition."

"I don't want to burden you Evelyn, but that would be wonderful. I think if I work hard, I can finish in two years and we can go back to Peru."

"Grade Point Average" seemed to be on every student's mind. "What's your GPA?" they would ask. "How did you do on the last test?" *I don't want to lose my faith and Christian experience over a GPA. From now on I'm going to spend 30 minutes with my Bible every night before going to bed. It won't matter how big the assignments or what test is coming up. I'll block out this time and spend it with God and His Word.*

Instead of losing out or getting behind, his grades actually improved. Still needing 124 semester hours of credits to graduate, he began looking for ways to speed up his education. After enrolling in summer school again, he signed up for a two-hour credit health science course through Home Study International.

The instructions were to send in no more than two lessons each week. To speed up the process, he did all the lessons at once and then sent them in two at a time. He enrolled in other courses and completed eight hours credit by home study.

One student told him it's possible to challenge a course by taking the final examination. He asked himself, *What knowledge have I gained in life that might apply to college work? Ah! I learned Spanish in Peru.*

He went to the language department and asked to take the exam for beginning Spanish. He passed in a breeze. "Now give me the intermediate Spanish test," he requested.

"Before you take that test, you must read a book on Spanish history," the instructor informed.

"No problem!" He read the book and passed the test. "Voilà!" he shouted. "This gives me 12 hours of Spanish credit."

He then asked to take the beginning German test. "Sorry, you can't do that. It's your native language."

"OK, let me do intermediate German." He passed and received an additional six hours credit.

"What else can I do?" he asked himself. He headed for the Industrial Arts Department and looked for the sewing section. The college women stared as he approached the teacher. "Madam, I'm a professional tailor from Berlin, Germany. I'd like to take the final test for any sewing class you offer here."

"Really! What do you have to show your experience in sewing?"

"Ma'am, my father's still wearing a suit I made. I can bring it tomorrow."

The next day, the instructor inspected his work. She asked questions about sewing practices she'd never seen before. Instantly he received four hours credit for sewing lab.

He went to the head of the carpentry department. "I'd like to get lab credit for my construction work. I built six buildings in the mission field."

The instructor asked, "Do you have pictures of your work?"

"Sir, I'll bring them tomorrow."

The teacher looked at pictures of the church and school Siegfried built at the Unini Mission Station. "That will give you credit for your lab work, but you'll have to take a written test. You'll be asked to design the roof for a ten story building with rafters cut off at the appropriate angle for a roof with a 5-foot rise."

Siegfried studied for a couple of days, came back, took the test, and passed. This gave him three hours more credit for a total of 25 hours challenged.

A few days later, he was called to the office of the Academic Dean. "Siegfried Neuendorff, who do you think you are? Do you think all you have to do is take tests and graduate. Sorry! Not at our school."

"Dr. Koenig," Siegfried protested, "I could have sat through the classes while studying something else, pass the tests, and even get GPA credit. I'm anxious to return to the mission field as soon as possible. If I get much older, the General Conference won't accept me."

"Oh, that's your problem. We will accept what you've challenged so far, but no more tests like these here on the La Sierra Campus."

"Thank you, Lord, for touching the dean's heart," Siegfried prayed as he walked out. *With 25 hours credit plus 8 more from home study, completing my degree in two years is a real possibility.*

Siegfried found Dr. Norskov Olson's class full of inspiration. At the same time, he struggled in a philosophy class with Dr. Fritz Guy. *What practical use will the philosophies of Descartes, Hume, Kant, Leibniz and Kierkegaard have for my future mission work?* Siegfried questioned. *I wish we could spend time learning how to conduct a church board meeting, hold a communion service, conduct a baptism, a wedding, or a funeral service.*

One thing Siegfried appreciated about Dr. Guy—he didn't require students to memorize. He said, "Any bird can do that. I want my students to think and verbalize their thoughts." In one exam, the question was asked: "How important is it for a student in modern times to study philosophy?"

In an effort to maintain his grade, Siegfried wrote: "A person in our time should have a broad education and be well informed." But he also added, "How many broken homes has philosophy united? How many hungry stomachs has philosophy filled? What is the work of philosophers? They seem to spend their lives criticizing those who preceded them. At the end, they either commit suicide or lose their minds." Siegfried determined "not to know anything … except Jesus Christ and Him crucified" (1 Corinthians 2:2).

Instead of the promised A, he got an A- in philosophy. But worse, when three of his brightest theology classmates became agnostics or atheists, he wondered, *Has all the long hours studying worldly philosophers robbed them of their faith?*

During his final semester at La Sierra, Siegfried and Evelyn were blessed by the birth of their son, Harold. He managed to arrange his schedule to be home when Evelyn worked. In spite of doing a lot of babysitting, he received five A's and one A- in philosophy. With the help of God, he had learned to study. His grade point average jumped from 2.22 to 3.23.

With graduation only two weeks away, Siegfried hurried home from classes. Evelyn handed him a letter from the General Conference. He tore it open. "Evelyn! It's an official call from the General Conference to go to Peru as full-time missionaries. They want us to work in the jungle town of Tarapoto on the Amazon side of the Andes." He hugged Evelyn. "You've been wonderful to work so I could study full time. God is answering our prayers!"

Siegfried also wanted to make communication easier in the future at mission sites when the need arose. *I've watched mission pilot Robert Seamount operate his Ham Radio at the Mission Air Base. I must get an amateur radio license.* He studied hard and passed the test. *Peru has reciprocity with the United States. I'll be able to use the U. S. License while working to get a Peruvian License.*

After taking his final examination at La Sierra, Siegfried walked out of the classroom and marched down the hallway shouting, "I'm finished, I'm finished! No more tests!" The following Sunday, his family watched him march to the platform of the Redlands Bowl and received his diploma as a theology graduate from Loma Linda University's La Sierra Campus.

After two stressful years of study, and being confronted by the College Dean for challenging so many courses, he didn't care much about graduation. Just one thought filled his heart with joy. *My family and I are going back to Peru to work for God in the Upper Amazon Jungle. The Lord has rewarded our efforts.*

Chapter 15
Rebel Missionary?

Siegfried held four airline tickets to Peru in his hand—his, Evelyn's, 10-year-old Eileen's, and one for baby Harold. He turned to Evelyn, "God has been good to help me complete my education. Now I understand why Pastor Pierson wanted us to become regular missionaries. Our tickets were purchased by the church. Jesus said, 'The laborer is worthy of his wages.' We must be faithful witnesses for the kingdom of God."

Church members from Tarapoto and Morales, along with representatives from nine organized groups, welcomed the Neuendorff family to San Martín in the Upper Amazon. A church leader helped them in getting a taxi to a rented house near the Tarapoto Church.

Siegfried looked inside—bare concrete floors. *What am I getting my family into?* The walls were unpainted—no cupboards, no closets, no shelves. No place to put anything. Church members loaned them three old wooden chairs, two older tables, and three mildewed mattresses.

Evelyn spoke. "We have lots of windows or we'd never stand the smell of these filthy mattresses." She spread out clean sheets thinking, *At least it's better than sleeping on the concrete floor.* She fixed a bed in a box for little Harold. Dim lights made night reading impossible.

Launching into his work, Siegfried discovered he would be preaching four new sermons every week. *Let's see,* he calculated, *my homiletics professor taught us that a good sermon needs 20 hours of preparation. I'll need 80 hours a week for study. Should I ask God for 36-hour days?* He realized that meeting the ideal in the mission field is not always realistic.

Visits to members' homes and Bible studies with interests took the major portion of time each day. Then someone was always knocking on their door needing help. Three weeks after arriving, a Pastor came from the Union Mission office.

Siegfried's stomach tied in knots when the visiting pastor pointed out all the things being done wrong. *What does he expect?* Before leaving, the pastor realized he'd been premature with his assessments. The new missionary was doing the very best under the circumstances.

Siegfried prepared grape juice planning to visit the nine groups under his care and conduct communion services. Before the weekend was over, the juice fermented and he was forced to cancel the last service. No one in Peru ever heard of Welch's grape juice, so after that he either carried fresh Concord grapes or raisins to prepare the sweet communion wine on location.

After many weeks, they received their shipment of household goods from the States. It included a Swan 500 CX single sideband amateur radio. Having received his Novice Amateur Radio License before leaving America, Siegfried told a church member about his desire to set up a station. Dr. Aquiles Lanao came to the Neuendorff home and offered to help.

This man was president of the local Peruvian Amateur Radio Club. He said, "We need more Ham operators in the jungle. I'll get you a license." A few days later, the license arrived. His call letters were OA9NQ. *I'm authorized to go on the air!*

The lot where they lived was too small for an antenna, so he made a deal with neighbors on both sides to attach the antenna between two coconut palms. Siegfried began calling "CQ, CQ, CQ, this is OA9NQ calling." He made calls to several countries. Suddenly a voice came on line, "What are you doing on this frequency?"

"I'm having a wonderful time," Siegfried replied. "I've just talked with Columbia, New Zealand, Ecuador, Panama, and three stations in the United States."

"Sir," the voice informed. "Your call letters tell me you're a novice and not allowed to be on the 20-meter band."

"I'm sorry! The president of the Amateur Radio Club didn't tell me anything about limitations when he gave me my call letters. I'll take down the antenna immediately and replace it with one for the 40-meter band," Siegfried promised.

The unknown operator said, "You will need to be on the air for six months and collect 100 QSL cards. Then you can apply for a General Radio License."

Siegfried had 100 cards ready to turn in when a visitor from Nebraska accidentally packed them in his luggage and left. *Why did this happen?* Siegfried fretted. However, pilot Clyde Peters helped Siegfried contact the man who walked off with his cards. When they finally arrived by mail, Siegfried prayed, "Thank you, Lord. You've helped me solve another problem." He took the cards to Dr. Lanao and applied for the General License. The license arrived by mail. His new call letters were OA9Q without the N, which stood for novice. Now he could use the 10-, 15-, 20-, 40-, and 80-meter bands.

When an earthquake shook the city of Moyobamba, the Neuendorff home became the center for official communication. Eight villages disappeared and 50 percent of 12 others were destroyed. Siegfried used his radio to make contacts that brought tents and blankets for families who lost their homes.

One day he heard two Ham operators discussing different types of antennas. He couldn't resist the temptation to break into the conversation. "Gentleman, I'm using a very special antenna here in the Amazon Jungle."

"What is it?" they wanted to know.

"It's a 'bi-coco' antenna."

"What's that? We've never heard of a bi-coco antenna."

"First you plant two coconut palms. Then you stretch your antenna between the trees and increase the coaxial cable each year as the trees grow taller." The men had a good chuckle.

Finding public transportation to meet appointments wasted a lot of time. After discussing the need for personal transportation with Evelyn, Siegfried purchased a 125cc Honda motorbike. Later he bought a used J-5 Jeep for $3,000. Townspeople called it the four-wheeled donkey.

The Jeep made it possible for the local church elder to accompany Siegfried on missionary trips. He also used it to help move members. It served in hauling sand and gravel for new church construction in Morales. It provided transportation for youth musical groups who took part in Siegfried's meetings. He used it to deliver donated clothing from the States to needy families. He hauled palm leaves to thatch a roof for a blind woman. More often than he wished, it served as a hearse. He'd also never forget the terrible stench when he hauled the bloated body of a man who drowned in the Huallaga River.

While serving in Nevati and Unini, Siegfried extracted more than 6,000 teeth. A city like Tarapoto had professional dentists. Checking with medical authorities, he learned he could only extract teeth where no dental services were available. An invitation came from Tabaloso: "Please come to our town and extract teeth." This would give him an opportunity to reach people that could never be reached in any other way. *But how can I fit this in my busy schedule?*

The mission encouraged workers to take Mondays off. *With my Jeep for transportation, I'll use my day off for this.* His service at that city brought an announcement over Radio Tropical the next day, saying. "Our city is grateful for the dental service given yesterday by the Adventist Church."

The mission pilot arrived in Tarapoto with an exciting update on the Unini Mission. "Do you remember the priest who showed up when you held meetings in Bolognesi? You gave him several magazines, *Steps to Christ, Ministry of Healing,* and *The Great Controversy.* Antonio Avanto has decided to be baptized and join the Seventh-day Adventist Church."

"Wonderful!" Siegfried exclaimed. "This encourages me to keep sowing the gospel seed."

After getting the Jeep, Siegfried asked God to guide in plans for evangelistic meetings in Morales. Driving into town for the first meeting, he noticed the entire town was dark—no electricity. *The devil must have something to do with this. I can't show pictures.*

Church members set up powerful kerosene lanterns. Soon, lights came on everywhere in town except at the crowded church. Siegfried preached anyway. In spite of a major problem on the opening night, people kept coming each evening and many made decisions to follow Christ.

Siegfried watched for every opportunity to witness. Church members became active and the work grew. When appropriate buildings were not available, he held meetings in public plazas or town squares.

Five months after the Neuendorffs returned to Peru, the new mission president, Pastor Itamar Paiva, came to their home. "Brother, Neuendorff," he began. "We're convinced the Holy Spirit is leading your life. Members of the churches and groups you serve appreciate your leadership."

"Thank you for your kind words," Siegfried responded.

The mission president continued, "We want you and your family to attend the Inca Union Mission Session scheduled six weeks from now at our college campus near Lima. We believe the Lord has called you to full-time ministry. We appreciate your dedicated family. Our mission committee has voted to recommend to the Union Committee that you be ordained to the gospel ministry during the coming session."

Siegfried drew a deep breath. "This is wonderful news. Ever since the train pulled out of a Berlin Railway Station taking me to a Hitler Youth Camp, I've prayed that God would guide my life. I've dedicated myself to God's service and will do my best to build up His kingdom."

On the final Sabbath afternoon of the Inca Union Mission Session, Siegfried stood with a large group of young ministers from Bolivia, Ecuador ,and Peru. They were asked to kneel for the ordination prayer and laying on of hands.

After the prayer, Siegfried listened to the charge: "Be an example to the believers in word, in conduct, in love, in spirit, in faith, in purity. … Give attention to reading, to exhortation, to doctrine. … Meditate on these things. … In doing this, you will save both yourself and those who hear you" (1 Timothy 4:12, 13, 15, 16).

The charge continued, "You are to preach the Word of God, not the opinions and traditions of men. You are to warn men and women of the soon coming of Christ. You are to preach so plainly that all who hear will understand the importance of the Law of God. Always remember that you are a messenger of the Lord, commissioned by Him to do a work, the influence of which is to endure throughout eternity.

"Your whole aim should be to bring sinners to repentance, pointing them to the Lamb of God which takes away the sin of the world.

"You have been solemnly dedicated to God by prayer and the laying on of hands. You are now authorized by the church to discharge all the regular functions of an ordained minister.

"I charge *you* … before God and the Lord Jesus Christ, Preach the word! … Convince, rebuke, exhort, with all longsuffering and teaching. … Be watchful in all things, endure afflictions, do the work of an evangelist, fulfill your ministry" (2 Timothy 4:1, 2, 5).

Determining to be faithful to the charge proved to be the most sacred moment in Siegfried's life. Next came the welcome presented by the Union President. "Welcome to the ranks of the gospel ministry. You are now a fully accredited Seventh-day Adventist minister. You are set apart by the church to a life of sacrificial service for Christ. I welcome you to its sorrows and its disappointments, its blessings and its joys. May God bless you in your service for Him."

Wives were invited to stand with their ordained minister husbands. *How fitting*, Siegfried thought. *Without Evelyn, I would not be here today. She's worked day and night meeting the medical and spiritual needs of church members. She's kept the church going and even preached sermons when I've been on trips. She's been willing to live anywhere and go anywhere.*

Our home has been a grand central station. She never complained about the hardships of jungle life. She hasn't fussed when insects, rats, and snakes invaded our home. She worked so I could study and complete the ministerial course. She did not complain about the isolation when we didn't get mail for weeks or months.

At the close of the service, they were introduced as Pastor Siegfried and Evelyn Neuendorff. On that happy day in January 1972, they little dreamed of the trials and trouble they would face in their service for God and their fellow men.

As a teenager in Berlin, Siegfried planned to spend his life sewing suits. As a minister, he would spend the rest of his life sowing the gospel seed. Newly ordained, he would continue sowing, but also experience the joy of reaping by baptizing converts to the faith.

Besides baptizing his own candidates, the mission asked him to baptize in Juanjui, Lamas, and Moyobamba. Twice Clyde Peters flew him to Panán where he baptized many Chayawita Indians. On trips outside his territory, he was frequently asked to conduct wedding ceremonies and baby dedications.

Segundo Misael raised his hand as Siegfried finished giving a Bible study in the city jail. "Pastor, I want to be baptized."

"Wonderful! Siegfried said. "You'll be getting out of jail in a few days. I'll arrange for you to be baptized in church."

"Pastor," Segundo insisted. "I know I'll be free in a few days, but I want to be truly free in Christ now. I don't want to wait to commit my life to God."

Since an attorney and an engineer, who were also inmates, wanted to witness the baptism, Siegfried asked the police for two bodyguards. The congregation waited reverently as police escorted an inmate into the church baptistry. Segundo buried his past sinful life in a watery grave.

Concluding the service, Siegfried asked, "How many here today want to prepare for a future baptism?" Six people responded including the attorney, his wife, and a secretary from the local bank. Siegfried found himself busier than every preparing candidates for heaven.

Words like "I want to be baptized" or "When will you baptize me?" brought joy to Siegfried's heart. The attorney, still an inmate at the city jail, continued to study. When he was finally released from jail, he brought friends to the pastor's house every week for Bible study.

There was Pablo Mori, the watchmaker; Abel Mory, head of the local Masonic Lodge; Angel Salinas, an instructor for the local Catholic Parish; and Arturo Bejar, controller at the local airport tower. The controller removed indecent pictures from his living room walls and asked his wife to dress simply without adornment. He even became a vegetarian. He sold his record player and stopped inviting friends for weekend dances. His neighbors complained, saying it was too quiet.

All these men recognized Bible truth but didn't accept it because of social commitments. The watchmaker asked, "Why are all your members humble people?"

The attorney, Juan Salazar, responded, "Here's one more humble person. Come and join me."

Before baptizing the Salazars, Siegfried asked them to leave the Masonic Lodge. "No one can serve two masters; for either he will hate the one and love the other, or else he will be loyal to the one and despise the other" (Matthew 6:24).

Siegfried came home one Sabbath evening and found Evelyn writhing in pain. "It's in the right side of my abdomen," she said, "But I don't think it is appendicitis."

Siegfried looked in her eyes. "They're yellow, dear. I think you have hepatitis. This is serious. We're going to the hospital."

By Sunday morning, her entire body turned yellow and they started giving IVs along with injections. The injections were so painful, she screamed, thinking, *This is nothing like Loma Linda.* She'd seen local people paralyzed after receiving the injections from poorly trained technicians. *Will I leave this place alive?*

The next time a technician came in she said, "I'm not taking any more shots." After three days of torture, she had enough. *This is terrible, but there's no other place to go. If I live or die, I'm in the Lord's hands.* She prayed, "Please Lord, may Your will be done."

With her new attitude, she began sleeping and a nurse introduced her to an Argentinean doctor who showed special interest in her case. At the end of a week, she was allowed to return home.

While visiting Evelyn in the hospital, Siegfried had a long conversation with a priest. Several days later, a church member sprang into Neuendorff's home. "What are you so excited about?" Siegfried asked.

"Listen to this! My wife and several others attended a class taught by a priest. He started criticizing different churches including his own. They're not Christians," he said. "They drink, smoke, party, and seldom attend church." He continued, "There's one church that's different. *Adventistas* live up to their principles. The pastor is kind, cheerful, and courteous. He was with his wife in the hospital the other day and we had a wonderful visit."

Siegfried smiled, "I talked with this man about getting victory over tobacco and alcohol. Let's pray that the Holy Spirit will continue working on his heart. Perhaps his kind words about our church will encourage others to recognize we have God's truth."

While conducting evangelistic meetings in the village of Juanguerra, Siegfried looked deep into his own heart. *I'm a hypocrite! I put on a good front, but inside it's often different. I'm sad, frustrated, miserable, and even a little disgusted.*

It started when the mission president spent several hours talking with him about his future work. "Brother Neuendorff, the Mission Committee voted to send you to work in Requena, on the banks of the Ucayali River."

"Pastor," Siegfried asked, "Do you mean I'm supposed to drop everything I'm doing in the Tarapoto District and start something completely new?"

"Yes, Brother Neuendorff. That's what the committee voted."

"Wait a minute. I've hardly been here two years. The groundwork's been laid. New groups of believers have been established. I have contacts with leaders in the community. Church members are supportive and the work is growing. Don't you leave a worker at his assignment for at least five years so he can see the results of his labor?"

The mission leader looked Siegfried in the eye, "And if we send you to Requena?"

"I won't go!" Siegfried blurted out without hesitation.

The mission administrator continued, "This is what we've been discussing with Union officers. Some think you're a rebellious worker."

Siegfried looked at the floor. *What am I hearing? God's blessing—the work is growing. Over 80 people have been baptized this year surpassing the mission goal. My district has a 70-percent tithe increase. I just received a letter from the Union President thanking me for our leadership. And now I'm a rebel. What's this all about?*

Siegfried listened to his superior. "You have a bad attitude Brother Neuendorff. When the mission takes an action, you need to accept it as the Lord's will."

Siegfried wanted to do the Lord's will, but he felt inexperienced men on the personnel committee were young and just beginning to learn the principles of sound administration. *They say this will solve a financial crisis and three workers will be laid off. Why abandon established work to begin something new? It doesn't seem like wise planning to me.*

Ugly thoughts continued to bounce around in Siegfried's mind. *If I'm a rebel missionary with a bad attitude, we might as well request a permanent return to the United States.* Then almost like a voice from heaven, "Siegfried, God brought you through trials before. He's still leading your life. Keep up your courage."

Later that week, Siegfried got on the radio and called the mission air base in Pucallpa. David Aguilar answered. "David Baasch, a General Conference Secretary is standing by my side. He wants to talk with you."

Interesting, Siegfried thought. *He's the one who processed all the paper work when we got our call to work in the South American Division.*

Pastor Baasch came on the radio asking, "How are you, Siegfried?"

"I'm absolutely miserable," Siegfried responded. He went on to explain his problems with the mission.

"But Siegfried," Pastor Baasch said. "I've been traveling around the Inca Union and I've only heard good reports about your work. I'm on my way to mission headquarters in Iquitos, so I'll check to find out what's going on."

Word arrived from the mission a few days later. "Effective January 1, in addition to the Tarapoto District, you will also be responsible for the Lamas District."

Siegfried gulped. *I'll need the Lord's help. Lamas has had their own pastor for 25 years. With 27 organized groups and four large churches, I will not be able to give them the attention they're used too.* His new territory compared in size to the Black Forest in Germany or all of the New England states in America.

Siegfried pressed forward as a good soldier for Christ. Every home in Tarapoto received a free copy of *Steps to Christ.* Officials of the cities where he worked received copies of *The Great Controversy.* He never hesitated to contact city mayors, police chiefs, army posts, school principals, hospitals, and jails.

After four years serving as a district pastor in San Martin, the Mission president announced, "Our recommendation that you have furlough during the first three months of the new year has been approved by the South American Division. When you return, you will be assigned to the Anna Stahl Clinic Church on the banks of the Amazon in Iquitos."

The president added, "You are a pioneer worker. God has given you the ability to reach people in the Middle and Upper Class. That's exactly what the church in Iquitos needs."

"Thank you for your kind words, Pastor. We just want to do our best wherever the Lord leads us."

Thank the Lord. He's not calling me a rebel. I wonder if we'll really get to Iquitos?"

Chapter 16

"You're a Spy"

"Siegfried, the phone's ringing. It's probably for you," Evelyn called during their furlough in California. Siegfried picked up the receiver. "Good morning, Brother Neuendorff. This is David Baasch at the General Conference. There's a change in plans. When you left Peru, they were asking you to return to Iquitos. The Inca Union Mission just voted to send you to Quillabamba in the South Peru Mission. Will you accept this change?"

"Just a minute, let me talk to my wife." In seconds Siegfried was back on the phone. "We've never heard of Quillabamba and don't know where it is, but if that's where God wants us, we will go." *It's easy to stand up in church on Sabbath morning and sing, "I'll go where you want me to go," but it's something else to put it into practice.* He asked Peruvians living around Loma Linda for information and no one had ever heard of the place.

All kinds of questions popped into his mind. *Why the change? Will we live in the city or country? What's the climate like? How many church members live in the area? Will I be able to use Amateur Radio?*

Arriving at their new destination, they discovered their home next to the church was the best they'd lived in during all their years in Peru. Quillabamba is located on the Vilcanota River in a lush tropical valley at about 5,000 feet in the eastern foothills of the Andes. The moderately warm climate with low humidity proved pleasant.

Siegfried and Evelyn were surprised to find only a small church congregation with 45 members and eight additional groups to pastor. It was certainly different than their previous district with four large churches and 27 active groups. *Why did God send us here instead of to Iquitos? Oh well, we will trust the Lord, because, "All* things *work together for good."*

Juan Velasco Alvarado, Peru's president at the time, held Marxist views and foreigners were looked on with suspicion. He planned to make ADRA illegal and expel the welfare arm of the church from his country. The morning he was to read his declaration, the country suffered a severe earthquake forcing him to cancel his plan. Peru needed the help ADRA could give.

People on the streets of Quillabamba, a city with 25,000 people, often challenged the new missionary to their valley. "Are you with the CIA?"

He sidetracked them saying, "I was born in Germany where we had the Gestapo, which is much worse than the CIA." One day while visiting the city jail, the guard said, "Your presence in our country is strange. Your posing as a missionary is a mask. No one else has a shortwave radio. Who knows what's hidden in your house?"

"Sir," Siegfried challenged. "Come to my house, check all the cupboards, look in all the nooks and crannies, see what you can find."

"But who knows what's hidden under your floor?" the man expressed his doubts.

Siegfried leaned over, cupped his hand next to the man's ear, and whispered, "Señor, under the floor, you'll find the sewer lines."

The guard broke up laughing and never asked the question again. Soon, however, Siegfried learned that the mayor's office was concerned and secret police were checking on him.

The Neuendorffs distributed 1,000 announcements for special meetings at the church. Back in Tarapoto, this would have brought out a large crowd, but Quillabamba had a different mentality. Only a few came. *Building personal friendships is the only way I will ever reach the public in this area.* He got permission to do dental work and offered to use his Amateur Radio to help in the event of any emergency.

Driving home one evening after holding meetings for a group of believes at Putucusi, a woman flagged him down. All out of breath she said, "Pastor, they just announced on the radio that you should go home as quickly as possible."

What's happening now? Are they asking all foreigners to leave the country? Has one of my children had an accident? Is there some special visitor who needs attention? Arriving home, he was told, "Go to the hospital, Evelyn's waiting for you there." He rushed to the hospital wondering what to expect.

Evelyn stood at the bedside of a 26-year-old Jewish woman from New York who broke her hip in a terrible auto accident while hitchhiking. "Get me out of here," Karen Wald pled.

The Neuendorffs recognized the little hospital was not equipped to take care of her serious injuries. Siegfried hesitated to give the young woman his name for fear prejudice against Germans would make her reject the help he could give. "Please call my uncle in New York, but ask him not to tell my parents my condition."

Siegfried rushed home and got on the short wave radio. The uncle promised to pay all expenses to get his niece back to the states. *But in her condition, she would not survive two hours over a rough gravel road and seven hours on the train. I've got to get a helicopter.*

With help from other Ham operators, he contacted Peru's Civil Aeronautics office in Lima. Bad weather delayed the chopper's arrival until the next morning. When Siegfried asked the police to clear the city's soccer field for a helicopter landing, one officer charged, "Helicopters don't land in Quillabamba. You're a spy for sure."

In the meantime, Siegfried had contacted a number of doctors asking instructions about the best way to transport the patient. Radio contact was made with Faucett Airlines to stand by for a stretcher patient arriving by helicopter. They refused. Quick thinking led to contact with the governor for the province of Cusco. "Sir, we have an international medical emergency and need your help."

"What do you want me to do?"

"Please order Faucett Airlines not to leave until the patient from Quillabamba is on board." The governor picked up his phone and called airport authorities and demanded they comply.

Soon the helicopter landed. Minutes later, Evelyn and her patient were placed on the Faucett flight. In the meantime, Siegfried arranged for Clinica Americana to have an ambulance ready for the patient's arrival. Evelyn stayed until the parents arrived from the United States to take their daughter home. She told her mom and dad, "We can be thankful for missionaries like the Neuendorffs. They saved my life."

The emergency evacuation brought Neuendorffs and the Adventist Church to the attention of local authorities. They asked Siegfried to serve as a member of the local Civil Defense Committee. He persuaded the chief of police to forbid the use of alcohol by all personnel involved in emergencies. A major and a lieutenant went to the Neuendorff home for Bible studies.

Segundo Díaz, known as the drunk corporal, accepted Bible studies and literature from Siegfried. Other police noticed that he stopped drinking and smoking. He and his wife went by the Neuendorff's house and asked about tithe. Immediately they began giving tithe. Finally, Segundo declared, "I can't stay in the police force and keep the Sabbath properly. I'm resigning and taking less pay to keep the Sabbath. My wife, Ruth, and I want to be baptized."

Siegfried's daughter Eileen, now 15, worked with other youth in the church to conduct evangelistic meetings. About 65 people attended every night. She gave Bible studies to several teenagers who were later baptized by her father. One Sabbath when her dad was away preaching, she gave the sermon in their home church.

When the owner of one of the city's two radio stations offered Siegfried free time on a daily basis, he initiated a radio program, *The Family Counselor*, featuring health, religion, and free Bible courses. Eileen told a children's story as part of each program.

⌒

Everyone in town knew his Jeep. He offered it as a prize to anyone who could show a text from Scripture that says we should worship on Sunday. The Catholic bookstore sold more Bibles that week than at anytime in its history. Folks were disappointed that no one won the Jeep, yet they learned an important truth—the text does not exist.

Soon people began greeting Siegfried with "Hello, family counselor." A third radio station opened in Quillabamba and the owner visited Siegfried offering free time for another program, meaning he now had four sermons and ten 30-minute radio programs to give each week. *What would my homiletics professor say now?*

Guido Valdivia from Radio Cultura attended a Friday evening meeting at the church to see pictures dealing with Creation and evolution. After the meeting, he said, " Siegfriedo [expression of endearment], you have wonderful material. The public needs to see and hear your messages."

"I've invited them, but they just don't come," Siegfried responded.

"It's true," Guido responded. "We live in a area where priests have damaged people's minds. Folks are taught it's the unpardonable sin to associate with a *Protestant devil*. We need to show people you aren't so bad after all. We must break down prejudice against foreigners and Protestants. Folks need to realize they don't have to go to confession after hearing you."

"How can we do this?"

"I'll arrange for you to give your presentations at the Agricultural Department's auditorium." Guido personally went on the air and began announcing the meetings. When they began, the large auditorium was packed. Ten minutes into the lecture, an employee asked Siegfried to stop. "What's wrong?"

"Señor, 500 people are pushing on the door trying to force their way in. Police have been called for crowd control."

"Help me know what to do now!" Siegfried prayed. He quickly had helpers place a large sheet on the outside of the building. The projector was placed on a table in the middle of the street and the lecture continued. Crowd control was no longer needed. Employees from the Agricultural Department asked for a program every two weeks.

At Easter time, Guido asked, "Siegfriedo, will you come to Radio Cultura and present the "Last Seven Words of Jesus on the Cross?" Realizing this is the custom in a Catholic community,

Siegfried got his material together and went to the station. *I'm surprised that the manager of a radio station with Marxist leanings would ask me to do this.*

He was ready to end when Guido signaled for him to continue. He was about to quit again when Guido again signaled, "Keep on. Don't stop now." Harold was there helping his dad organize cassettes for the background music. "Son, please run home and bring me *The Desire of Ages*." Siegfried then read chapters dealing with the Passion. In total, he broadcasted for over eight continuous hours. A woman approached Siegfried on the street the next morning. "You had me crying as I listened to your program last night."

"I have to admit," Siegfried said, "I shed tears too. It's wonderful to know what Jesus has done for us." The next year, Guido gave him 11 hours of continuous broadcasting.

The Roggero family, teachers from the public school system, stopped by the Neuendorff's home accompanied by their adult daughter whose husband served as a Peruvian Air Force pilot. They wanted to know if it would be possible to contact her husband by Ham radio. Siegfried tried, but was unable to get a response.

Although the radio contact proved unsuccessful, they talked about spiritual things for the next hour and a half. Two days later, on the way to visit the jail, Siegfried met the Roggeros parked on the street. After talking for half an hour, they invited him to their home for Bible study at 4:30 in the afternoon the next day.

When the Bible study finished, Santiago Roggero asked, "If we died, or if Jesus came right now, would we be ready?"

What a question! Siegfried thought a moment and speaking kindly said, "My friends, I don't think so, but God wants you to be ready! I'll be back to study more."

"Thank you, Don Siegfriedo. No one ever talked to us about the Bible the way you have. Your enthusiasm is contagious."

On the third visit to the Roggero home, the parents sat down with their very attractive daughter, who was dressed in very tight shorts and a revealing top. *What am I doing trying to give a Bible study teaching people to be ready for heaven and I keep staring at this girl? I'm a minister and I need to keep my mind pure.*

A battle waged in Siegfried's mind. Finally, he turned to the girl and as tactfully as possible, said, "I'd like to ask a big favor.

God gave you a very attractive body, and I want to keep my mind on God's Word. Would you be willing to go out and put on some modest clothing?"

While the young woman went to change, he apologized to the parents. "It's not a problem," they said. "You did the right thing." When the girl came back, she was appropriately dressed.

Did I do the right thing? What would Jesus have done? Should I have simply ignored the girl, but how could I when she was right in front of me? Is it me or the girl who did wrong? God's Word says, "If I regard iniquity in my heart, the Lord will not hear" (Psalm 66:18). Yet the awkward encounter did not dampen the enthusiasm of the Roggero family. They continued studying three times a week.

A few weeks later, they stopped by the Neuendorff home. "Pastor, we've been transferred to another school for the new school year. The Holy Spirit is changing our lives. We're going to our new assignment with a new vision of how God wants us to live. Thank you for the time you've spent with us. We'll be by to see you when we come to get our monthly paycheck. Thank you for teaching us about repentance, faith, and willing obedience. We want to learn more of God's wonderful truth." *Praise the Lord! There's no joy like seeing men and women place their faith and trust in the Savior.*

At the new school, the Roggeros were challenged by the priest for not making the sign of the cross during public prayer. They defended their position saying, "Pastor Siegfriedo taught us what the Bible says about prayer. We plan to be baptized and join the Adventist Church."

After their baptism, they approached Pastor Neuendorff. "Thank you for teaching us the truth. A heavy burden has been taken from us." When former friends abandoned them, they said, "It doesn't matter. Our faith in Jesus Christ fills our hearts with peace and joy." Their daughter even looked up the Adventist Church in Lima.

The first big test came only a few days after their baptism. Santiago was told, "You are being relieved of your responsibilities here and will be transferred to another school. From now on you and your wife will not be teaching at the same institution." This weighed on his mind as they traveled to Lima to visit their daughter. During a medical checkup, the doctor reported, "Santiago, you need surgery to remove a tumor." Would these difficulties lead them to give up their new faith?

A few weeks later, Santiago stood with his wife in the Quillabamba Church. "I want to thank the Lord for a pastor who taught us God's truth. He showed from the Bible the importance of returning tithe. This was tough for me to put into practice. I didn't think I could do it."

The congregation listened attentively. "Friends, the Lord returned my first tithe 10 times over. The doctor in Lima said my surgery would cost 50,000 *soles*, but he decided not to charge me one *centavo* [penny]. In the evening, another doctor brought all the medicines I needed free. That's not all. Early this morning, the coordinator from the Educational Department came and told me I will not lose my job or be transferred. Instead, the person who caused the trouble has been removed from his post. My wife and I will continue teaching in the same school!"

Siegfried and Evelyn struggled with an educational problem of their own. Evelyn had stayed busy helping people, but Eileen, now 17, completed the eleventh grade by correspondence. *It's time to send her to the states to complete her education.*

Sending a minor back to the states required a lot of time-consuming documentation including tax declarations. An accountant worked for more than four hours preparing the document. When Siegfried tried to pay, the accountant smiled, "How can I charge anything when you're the pastor of my future church?"

In a short time, Eileen was on a plane flying to the United States leaving her parents with an anxious feeling in the pit of their stomachs. *What kind of cultural shock will our daughter face? How will she do living with grandparents? How will she face peer pressure?* God answered their secret prayers. Eileen studied hard, passed the GED, and entered La Sierra University in the fall.

Two Adventist teenage girls living in Quillabamba during their final year at high school were informed, "Your final examinations will be given on Saturday." *What are we going to do? If we fail to take the test, we'll lose our entire year and not graduate.*

When they asked for counsel, Siegfried responded with a question. "What is more important? To obey God or man? Graduation, or a home in heaven?"

"We see the point," the girls exclaimed. "We will not take examinations on God's holy Sabbath." Siegfried prayed with the girls asking the Lord to work out His will for them. Placing their faith in Christ, the girls attended church on Sabbath. God answered their prayer by impressing the professor to reschedule the tests for the following Wednesday.

The next week, two visitors—the daughter of the head of the Evangelical Church and her husband—walked into a Friday night meeting at the church. *Why are they here?* Siegfried wondered. They looked extremely sad.

The couple approached Siegfried at the end of the meeting. "Pastor, will you come to our house and pray for our little girl?" As Siegfried and Evelyn accompanied these parents to their home, the couple recounted, "Several months ago our daughter died with a high fever. Now our younger daughter's just spent five days in the hospital burning up with a high fever. All the antibiotic injections have failed to produce results." Holding back tears, the parents continued, "Doctors say there is nothing more they can do for her and asked us to bring her home. We can't believe God wants us to lose another child."

Siegfried and Evelyn hurried to the home where they found the entire family standing around the girl's bed. Thinking she was going to get another injection, the daughter cried when Evelyn touched her arm. "This girl's burning up with a raging fever," she whispered to Siegfried. They asked for a pan of warm water.

After the bed bath and words of comfort for the family, Siegfried invited everyone to kneel for prayer. "Dear, Lord, as Creator, You made this little girl. You know this family's anxiety. You are the Great Physician. You died to save this helpless child and You know what is best for her. If it's Your will, please touch her body and heal her, I pray in the name of Jesus."

The Neuendorffs stayed with the family until midnight. The next evening, the young couple walked into the meeting with big smiles on their faces. "Please come to our house and pray again. We want to thank God for a miracle. Our daughter woke up this morning and jumped out of bed asking for breakfast. The terrible fever's gone."

"Praise the Lord," Siegfried said. The Lord rewarded your faith." The parents brought the child to Sabbath school and worship services."

~~~~~

Sometime later, mission administrators arrived in Quillabamba to assess the needs in the area. After auditing church financial records, the treasurer said, "I'm amazed how tithe and offerings have increased."

Siegfried invited the president to visit the police station and talk to men who were responsible for law enforcement. He joined in a dialogue at one of the two radio stations where Siegfried had daily programs. On Sabbath afternoon, he witnessed a baptism.

The men were about to leave when the president indicated they would like to talk with Siegfried and Evelyn alone. "We've watched your work. Everyone in town knows you. We haven't seen anything like this anywhere else. You've complained saying you don't believe in goals and that a worker should simply do his best and leave the results up to God. We've noticed though that you always reached your baptismal goals."

"I still don't believe in goals that put pressure on a worker," Siegfried responded. "All that's happened here is the result of God's blessing. The Lord gets all the credit."

The men from mission headquarters continued: "We believe God wants us to start new work in Arequipa. It's the largest city in our mission and we've never done anything like you are doing here. Will you accept a call to come to mission headquarters in Arequipa and serve as Communication and Health Director? You could help us establish a shortwave radio network so we can keep in touch with all areas of our large mission."

The news hit like a bolt of lightening. *Shall I accept this challenge?* He and Evelyn spent a lot of time together on their knees. Before the men left the next day, Siegfried told them, "The Lord has guided our lives. If you believe a move to Arequipa is God's will, we will accept and do our best."

The men explained, "You've been here five years and we're asking the South American Division to give you a 10-month furlough according to church policy. You will have six months to finish your work here. Before you go, you can store your belongings at Mission Headquarters in Arequipa.."

The leaders left. Siegfried immersed himself in his work. *With only six months to finish my work in Quillabamba, I must make every minute count for Christ.*

Chapter 17
"Papa Loves You"

A messenger came running from Quillambamba's post office at suppertime. Out of breath, he said to Siegfried, "Turn on your Ham radio immediately." Making contact with a radio colleague, he listened to an emergency message from Mutti. "Siegfried, come home to California. Your father's very ill!" *What's wrong? My father's been a strong man all his life.*

The next morning, he caught the first train to Cusco. During the long ride, he had plenty of time to think. *Since I was a child, Papa downgraded every thing I did. He made fun of me, called me stupid—for him I could never do anything right. When I chose to become a tailor, he said it was degrading. When we decided to come to Peru as volunteers, he said I was throwing my life away. He attended my graduation from theology with Mutti, but never said one word of congratulations. I learned to live without Papa's approval, but fortunately there's a happy ending.*

The year before, Siegfried's parents accepted his invitation to visit him and his family in Peru. He arranged to fly them in the mission plane to the Unini Mission Station and many of the other places where he'd worked in the jungle. His parents went to church with him and listened to him preach in Spanish. They watched him gently extracting teeth from suffering natives. They listened to his daily radio broadcasts.

Siegfried took them to visit the famous Inca Ruins of Machu Picchu. Traveling on the narrow gauge railway between Cusco and Quillabamba, Mutti poked Siegfried's father. "Now you tell Siegfried what you wanted to say."

"No!" Papa insisted. "You tell him for me."

Siegfried couldn't imagine what his parents were discussing and was hardly prepared for what he was about to hear. "Siegfried," his mother began. "Papa asked me to tell you he loves you and he's very proud of the work you are doing in Peru."

Siegfried could hardly believe his ears. *For 43 years I've waited to hear a word of approval from my father. Now in tenderness, he can't say what he wants to say, so he has Mutti say it for him. At last I know my father's attitude toward me has changed. Praise God!*

The train jerked to a stop in Cusco, and Siegfried hurried to the airport and caught a flight to Lima with hopes of making a connection to Los Angeles. Only a few weeks before, Siegfried wrote to his father telling the joy of seeing the transformation in the life of a teacher, who after postponing a commitment to the Lord for years, finally made a decision to be baptized. Then he challenged his father: "How about you, Papa? Are you willing to take that step too? My family prays for you and my brother every morning at worship. We want you to have both physical and spiritual health. With God's blessing, you can be with us for a long time and be prepared for the world to come. You're not just another person. You are my special Papa. You taught me the principles of life that have made me the person I am. I want to be with you in heaven."

Was I too strong in appealing to my father? I just pray he's committed his life to Christ without reservation.

After arriving in Los Angeles, Siegfried stood by Papa's bedside in ICU at the Loma Linda University Medical Center. All kinds of IVs and monitors where hooked up to his body. He'd survived surgery in which two thirds of his small intestines were removed.

In spite of massive amounts of antibiotics, he developed a fungus infection on his diaphragm. Siegfried spoke softly as he leaned closer to his father's ear. "Papa, I've come to see you." With an oxygen mask over his mouth, it was impossible for Papa to respond. He simply nodded, indicating he recognized his son and understood. In order not to interfere with medical personnel, Siegfried stayed only a few minutes.

Each morning he and his mother went to give encouragement to his father and pray with him. Siegfried answered when the phone rang at five in the morning on Sabbath. "This is Dr. Briggs. Come immediately if you want to see your father alive."

Mutti and Siegfried rushed to the hospital. Papa's heart stopped three times and each time electric shock got it going again. Finally at noon, his heart stopped again. Dr. Briggs asked, "What do you want us to do? Keep on giving electric shocks?"

Siegfried turned to his mother to hear her wishes. "His heart and body are tired," they told the doctor. "Just let him rest." Mother and son stood together in silence. Siegfried thought, *I'm so glad I wrote asking him to accept Christ. I hope he made a positive response. I'll find out when Jesus comes.*

After the grave side service, Siegfried asked Mutti, "How long do you want me to stay with you? A week? A month? Till the end of the year?"

Frank and outspoken as ever, she said, "The reality will hit me, but you may as well go back now. Your work for God must go on. Eileen is here and I will be all right."

"Mutti," Siegfried said. "I'll be praying the Lord will be with you to give you comfort at this difficult time. Our furlough begins in April, so we will be back to help you in any way we can." That evening Siegfried got a flight back to Peru.

⁓

Arriving in Lima, he tried unsuccessfully to contact Evelyn to let her know he was safe in Peru. Finally he got the Civil Defense Department to relay his message. They got through all right, but the message Evelyn received was, "Your husband passed away." Evelyn and Harold worried until Siegfried walked in the front door.

Membership at the Quillabamba Church increased each year the Neuendorffs stayed. The church was filled with active young people who truly loved the Lord. But the situation in the town deteriorated because of increased drug trafficking. Not only were the streets filthy, but crime increased greatly, making life dangerous.

Someone stabbed a police officer. A young boy lost an eye for failing to cooperate with thugs. A man, walking with his wife near the cemetery, was stabbed in the abdomen. Two men held a knife at the throat of a young woman who took Bible studies. Discovering she had no money, they began pulling her clothes off until a car appeared and they ran away. People on the street were often robbed at gunpoint.

Yet too soon the day came for the Neuendorffs to leave. "You've been a real friend," church members said. "You've given us a new direction in our lives. We'll miss you very much."

Tears filled his eyes when Siegfried prayed, "God bless these dear people and keep us all faithful as part of Your great family."

Back at Loma Linda, Siegfried discovered his mother doing well in spite of her great loss. It also gave them satisfaction to find their daughter completing her first year of college at La Sierra. After attending the General Conference Session in Dallas, Texas, as official delegates, they were invited to tour churches in West Germany.

Before leaving Germany, they visited East Berlin. Entering communist territory proved extremely uncomfortable. The very few automobiles on the streets were all painted gray. Streets were practically empty except for police stationed everywhere. They could hardly wait to get back to the west. In West Berlin, Siegfried showed his family the old house where he was born 47 years earlier.

Although church leaders approved a 10-month furlough, Siegfried grew restless. Leaving their daughter at La Sierra, and telling Mutti goodbye, they returned to Peru after only six months.

Life at 8,000-feet in Arequipa, Peru's second largest city located at the foot of volcano El Misti, proved to be another challenge. Mission officers promised them an apartment with four bedrooms and four bathrooms. Instead they were asked to move in with Ruth Sonoco, a mission secretary living in a tiny apartment. They shared the bathroom and tiny kitchen. She slept in the small bedroom and they shared the living room with their son Harold.

Then what was supposed to be only a few days turned out to be seven months. Siegfried and Evelyn agreed: *Ruth is a saint to put up with us for so long.*

With the year coming to an end and a shortage of pastors, mission administrators asked Siegfried to travel to cities where folks waited to be baptized. One destination was Quillabamba, where he'd just worked for five years. When 2,000 people attended a meeting he conducted in the main plaza, he realized his time spent in this city was not in vain.

During his first long trip, Siegfried baptized dozens of people including a 103-year-old man. Back at the office as Public Relations and Health Director, he contacted City Hall, the police department, students at the National University of San Augustín, the Technological Institute, the sanitation plant, city water plant, the local jail, the general hospital, and several high schools.

First, he presented strictly temperance lectures and films. Soon, however, folks began asking for religious topics too. Even though he'd been asked to pastor a large church, along with his departmental responsibilities, a new idea popped into Siegfried's head. He offered his services to Channel 6 Television. The manager said, "Let's show one of your films to our program director." She and the manager loved the film, *Countdown*. "Go talk with our administrator," they advised. The administrator leaned back in his chair. "If the manager approves it, you're on!"

Each 30-minute film would be followed by a 10-minute discussion with professional people and Siegfried as moderator. They set the date for the first program. Siegfried walked out of the TV station. *Now what am I going to do? No one ever taught me how to do a television show!*

Siegfried prepared double-spaced scripts for the program director and cameraman. He invited an Adventist physician, the Chief of Transit Police, and the head of Cultural Activities for the City of Arequipa to serve on his panel for the program titled *Tobacco and Your Health*. During the hour-long show, people began calling in expressing their appreciation.

He was leaving when a woman called saying, "My husband's a heavy smoker and needs to see this. Could you repeat the program?" Immediately the program director set a date for a program rerun.

When Siegfried walked into the mission office the next morning, he was greeted by the president. "You didn't tell us what you were doing, but we were proud of you last night. We praise God for the thousands who were reached."

This was the beginning of 32 additional programs shown on prime time at no cost to the church. Soon similar TV programs were aired in the other major cities of the mission. When Siegfried visited schools, children always asked, "Are you the man on television?"

An encouraging letter arrived from the Union Mission Office: "Congratulations for being the first to air an Adventist program live on TV in Peru. Please make this a school to teach others to use TV to reach the masses."

Arequipa's mayor insisted on charging 3.5 million *soles* to issue a building permit to rebuild a church destroyed by an earthquake. When church leaders asked for a discount, he asked, "What are you doing for the city?"

"Our church sponsors Siegfried Neuendorff with free lectures on health and temperance. He's conducted programs for all your city employees and has been reaching out to all via television." Immediately the mayor ordered all fees for the permit canceled.

The television programs brought dozens of requests for health and temperance lectures. The managers of two bus lines asked for presentations on alcohol and the family. A military colonel asked for temperance programs for army recruits. Even the Coca Cola Company asked for lectures for their 250 employees.

The archeology class at the local Catholic University asked for a lecture on *Evolution vs. Creation*. When the General in charge of the Secret Police called for Siegfried, he wondered, *What kind of trouble am I in now?* The General simply asked, "Will you come and show films on the danger of drugs and alcohol for a special session of Boy Scouts?"

Siegfried, happy for more opportunities to witness than he could possibly handle, didn't dream his bubble was about to burst. Enrique Baerg, the Union President, visited his office during a year-end meeting. He almost shouted, "Neuendorff, you're not doing the work we assigned you to do. All your contacts with the public are worthless! You are just going around and doing nothing for the church."

Saddened to hear a leader talk like this, Siegfried's eyes filled with tears. *I thought everything I'm doing was for the church?* Between sobs, he said, "Yes, Pastor, I've been reaching out to the public, but every Sabbath I'm speaking in a church." He quickly pulled out a report of his work for the year showing that besides preaching every Sabbath, he'd conducted weeks of health and temperance emphasis in many churches."

"But we don't want that," Pastor Baerg insisted. "You should have trained others to do that."

"I'm sorry Pastor Baerg, but no one ever gave me a job description. Leaders from the General Conference and Division have affirmed my work. The mission president told me to continue what I'm doing. Leaders in the city seem to think that we only work for the poor. I've tried to change that image and reach the upper classes too. If what I'm doing is not satisfactory, I can work in Canada, or Germany, or the USA."

Suddenly Pastor Baerg's attitude changed. "No! We need you here!" He thanked Siegfried for sharing his frustrations and assured him of support from church leadership.

Living in a city with ample dental service, Siegfried hadn't extracted a tooth for a long time. One day, Harold's orthodontist indicated one of his molars needed removing to leave space for the rest of his teeth. At the same time, Evelyn had problems with three molars. Why pay a dentist? Siegfried got out his equipment and extracted the teeth without a problem.

The live television programs brought many strangers seeking marriage counsel to Siegfried's office and to their home. He and Evelyn spent many hours trying to mend troubled homes. Women complained about unfaithful husbands and physical abuse. Men claimed they had too many children and it's the wife's fault. Many were sexually abused. Children were beaten with belts or other household articles. With the Lord's help, the majority of homes planning to break up decided to give it another try and stayed together.

Fifty Sabbath-keeping youth faced a major problem. The National University of San Augustín where they planned to attend scheduled the entrance examination on Sabbath. They went to Siegfried seeking help. He took the group of youth to visit the president of the university.

On the way, a professor who had invited Siegfried to speak at the Catholic University stopped him to say hello. "What are you doing here?" He wanted to know.

"We're on our way to see the university president."

"Oh, I'm going there too."

"By any chance, are you a member of the Admissions Committee?

"Yes, I am, but why do you ask?"

Siegfried explained the dilemma faced by the students. An hour later, he still waited with the students for the president to return from committee. Suddenly folks began leaving the committee, and the professor they met on the way in came straight to Siegfried. "Your problem is solved," he said. "Simply write a request to cover all your students. We voted to let them take the exam on another day."

"Wonderful! Praise the Lord!" Siegfried turned to the students. "God solved your Sabbath problem. Now it's up to you to prepare well. I will find teachers who are specialists and offer special classes to help you."

While waiting for his baggage after a long bus trip from Tacna, Siegfried asked a driver, "Have you seen me before?"

"Yes, Sir," the man responded. "You gave health lectures and showed health films here at the bus station. And you know what? Two drivers who were heavy drinkers aren't drinking any more."

"Wonderful," Siegfried exclaimed. "And I'm sure they are happier too."

A woman approached Siegfried, "My husband and I visited you for counsel. We are so much happier now. I'm trying to do my part in helping my husband."

Siegfried, completely immersed in his work reaching out to people, received news he was being transferred to Peru's capital city, Lima. He would be doing the same kind of work for the Central Peru Conference. But the work there would be some of the most dangerous in his life.

Their new neighbors drove a Mercedes 280 SL and owned a ritzy restaurant. Soon after moving in, they heard a woman screaming at 2:30 A.M. Running outside, they discovered the neighbors wife had jumped on their roof to get away from her drunk husband who was trying to kill her with a machete.

Driving to a speaking appointment one evening, he saw four drunks who'd been hit by passing cars lying on the pavement. Siegfried put the three worst in his Jeep. Police arrived and picked up the fourth. The patrol car led the way with flashing lights all the way to the nearest hospital.

Harold attended the local Adventist Academy. After school one day, two thugs grabbed him by the back of the neck and tried to take his watch and money. The boy stayed calm and told the men they'd better watch what they were doing. The assailants let him go. The Neuendorffs thanked the Lord for protecting their son.

Carmen Escalente, a faithful church member, had a burden to reach Lima's higher class. Her efforts brought invitations for Siegfried to speak to the Army, Air Force, Navy, Republican Guard, and Secret Police. He conducted seminars at several universities including the University of San Marcos, the oldest in South America. Large companies, like the Paramonga Sugar Company with 1,000 employees, asked for lectures against alcohol and tobacco.

Siegfried conducted seminars reaching a total of 9,600 police officers. His topics included *Secrets of a Happy Home, Dangers of Alcohol, Tobacco and Drugs,* and *The Education of Children.* He always ended with the most important message of all, *A Safe Guide for Your Life,* showing how the Bible could lead them to experience joy and happiness. Finally, he offered his listeners the opportunity to enroll in the Voice of Prophecy Bible Course.

Melchor Feyerra, a young pastor who later became president of the Peruvian Union Mission, arranged for Siegfried to speak to 2,500 employees at a mine. The head of social services for the mine contacted Pastor Feyerra saying, "After two days of lectures, the industrial accident rate dropped. Fewer called in sick, production increased, and incidents of family problems were reduced. We'll be delighted to welcome Siegfried Neuendorff back any time."

Devaluation of Peruvian money led to serious problems for mission workers. Siegfried showed his latest paycheck to Evelyn. "Look at this, Dear. We're millionaires!" The large check for over one million *soles,* worth only $155, made it difficult to survive.

The news constantly reported shootings of innocent people by the *Sendero Luminoso* [Shinning Path], a dangerous group of terrorists. Two men were asked to give up their faith. One denied his faith. The other stood firm and was taken to the main plaza in the center of town and shot in the head. At another place they killed 40 farmers.

Seven lay church leaders stood in the dark with their backs to the wall of the church where they worshipped. Cold winds off the glacier Ausangate, high in the Peruvian Andes, whipped around the church, chilling their faces. In silence they faced a group of Shining Path guerrillas who disguised themselves in typical Indian clothing. The firearms they carried were hidden beneath long heavy ponchos.

Earlier that evening, the terrorists pounded on the door of the adobe thatched roof hut where the head elder of a Quechua Adventist Church lived. The Shining Path group cursed when they found only the wife and children at home. The fortunate elder was attending an evangelistic meeting 20 miles away.

Next on their hit list was the home of another elder. They dragged him out in the dark night and forced him to accompany them to the house of the church youth director. He too was forced to leave his family. Next they went to the house of the church treasurer. When he tried to resist, he felt the point of a gun through the heavy wool fabric of a guerilla poncho. In a short time, seven church leaders were rounded up and marched to their church. Children and wives, concerned for their fathers and husbands followed.

The seven men stood quietly in the dark night with their backs to the church wall. The guerilla leader ordered them to shout, "Long live the Shining Path! Long live the revolution! Down with religion!" These seven Seventh-day Adventist men stood with their mouths closed listening to insults by these wicked men. "Your refusal to join with us shows you are loyal capitalists. You are nothing but a bunch of religious parasites." The wives who had followed fell on their knees and with tears pled with the terrorists not to harm their husbands.

The leader faced the men against the wall and spoke roughly. "I want to make it very clear. Forget this religious nonsense and join in our battle to destroy the government of Peru or you die tonight."

Seven humble men responded kindly, "We must be faithful to our God. We must love Him and keep His commandments. We will not join your revolution."

The angry guerilla leader called the men to attention. The terrorists reached for the weapons hidden under their ponchos, and the sound of gunshots filled the night air. Tearful wives, with children by their sides, watched courageous husbands tumble and fall, bathed in blood from gunshot wounds. The guerrillas vanished in the night, leaving the mothers and children to weep over the loss of husbands and fathers.

These men paid with their lives staying faithful to Jesus. The families could only trust in a promise the slain men had known well. "Be faithful unto death and I will give you the crown of life" (Revelation 2:10). The next day with the help from other church members the seven stricken families buried their dead.

Shining Path guerrillas plagued Peru for more than 10 years. They learned that Adventist Churches sent tithe to the mission headquarters each month. In several remote areas, they demanded that the money be given to them to promote the revolution. Adventist believers consistently responded that the only worthwhile *revolution* is when Christ gets into the hearts of men and women and transforms their lives through the power of the Word of God.

In one 12-month period, 19 church leaders were assassinated for their faith. In Lima, where the Neuendorffs lived, frequent blackouts caused by terrorist activities often left the city in chaos. Foreigners were often threatened.

After 20 years in Peru, it would be difficult to leave people they loved, but Siegfried needed to face reality. Four things weighed on his mind as he considered his family's future: Harold's education—his son needed to go to college; his aging mother needed attention; Eileen planned a summer wedding and wanted her father to conduct the ceremony; the deteriorating political situation in Peru.

After much earnest prayer, Siegfried and Evelyn decided to make plans to return to the United States. At the end of the 1984, he wrote a letter of resignation and handed it to the conference president who read it immediately. "Do you really mean this?"

"Yes," Siegfried replied. "It's been a tough decision because we love our work with the wonderful Peruvian people. We must get home in time for our daughter's wedding, but we will keep doing our best here until then."

Culture shock on returning to the States after so many years overseas proved a challenge. They loved the orderly traffic, but wondered why everyone seemed so consumed with things. Huge supermarkets were filled with so many tempting foods and made it difficult to know what to buy. Still, Siegfried continued working for the Lord by pastoring churches at Redondo Beach, Culver City, Pomona, and Huntington Park.

Suddenly, a new millennium dawned, the beginning of the twenty-first century. Siegfried looked back at his life. *My worst year was spent in a Hitler Youth Camp. Twenty of the best years were serving as a missionary to Peru. Fifteen challenging years followed as a pastor in Southern California.*

He talked with Evelyn. "God has blessed me for 66 years. It's time to retire."

But retirement is relative. He held outreach meetings in Russia. He's also returned to Peru several times to hold evangelistic meetings. He stays active giving Bible studies and helping in churches wherever needed. As always, the Lord's work goes on in silent prayer and with earnestness.

Chapter 18
The Empty Lot

J ust weeks short of turning 96, Mutti died in Siegfried's home the same year he retired from full-time pastoral duties. Standing by her grave side next to where he buried Papa 20 years earlier, Siegfried prayed silently, "Thank You for a mother who taught me to love the Lord. She sacrificed much to make sure our family had food when none was available. She gave me her own winter coat and walking shoes when none could be purchased for me."

Siegfried will never forget his brave mother. With the war at its worst, she faced Frau Friederich at the Hitler Youth Camp in Poland, announcing, "I've come to take my son."

"Never!" Frau Friederich insisted. "Your son belongs to the German government. He must stay here."

What a woman. If she hadn't literally stolen me away and put me on the last train out of Poland, I wouldn't be here today. The other boys in that camp were never heard from after the war ended.

Two years into the twenty-first century, Siegfried began reviewing God's leading in his life. "Evelyn," he said, "Let's visit my birthplace one more time. It's been 69 years since Hitler came to power and I was born. During long nights hiding in bunkers while bombs exploded outside, I prayed for survival. During the lonely year at a Hitler Youth Camp, I prayed to see my parents again. Today I'm praying God will keep us ready for the soon coming of Jesus."

Siegfried's pulse jumped as their plane touched down in Berlin. During his short visit 22 years earlier, the city was only an island in a huge communist sea. The Berlin Wall made it difficult to reach relatives in East Berlin. Now they found a booming city in a united

Germany. The 97-mile wall, dividing the city for 28 long years, was gone. Berliners spontaneous explosion of joy when the wall came down is somewhat negated by the fragile economy and unemployment in the East, which still remains a challenge for Germans to solve.

On the bright side, Berlin is again the capital of Germany and the largest industrial city in Europe. New construction is everywhere. Debris from World War II destruction has been turned into parks. Streets are crowded with a generation who no longer remember the dark days of war during the Hitler regime.

On the first Sabbath back in Berlin, Siegfried spoke at his old home church. Memories of becoming a member of the Mariendorf Adventist Church on Koblenzer Strasse after his baptism at age 13 flooded his mind. *I never dreamed I'd be preaching in this church. When I was baptized, I could not imagine I would have the privilege of baptizing my own children.* He marveled at what God had done.

He baptized his daughter Eileen when she turned 13 while living in the Upper Amazon at Tarapoto. As a small child, this precious girl loved Jesus and always took part in religious activities helping her parents in every way she could. Today she serves with her missionary husband at an Adventist Medical Clinic on the Island of Okinawa.

Her brother, Harold, 10 years younger, was very different. Living with parents who were always involved with church, prayer meetings, evangelism, Bible studies, producing Christian radio programs, family worship—Siegfried worried that his son might be getting too much religion. For a while, the boy didn't want to pray, but his parents prayed for him.

When Evelyn was on a trip to Cusco with Eileen, Harold looked at his father while they ate together and suddenly asked, "What would we do if Mama and Eileen died?"

"Well, you'd have to live with me. Wouldn't you like that?" Siegfried asked.

He felt like a knife pierced his heart when his son responded, "No! You bother me too much!"

What is going on with this child? What am I going to do? Siegfried worried, but kept on praying. The food Siegfried prepared was nothing like Evelyn's cooking, so naturally Harold wouldn't want to live without his mom. The Holy Spirit touched his life in a different way.

A few months later, Harold marched into his father's office, stood in front of his desk, and looked straight at his dad. "Papa," he said. "I want to study the Bible."

Siegfried listened in amazement. "Harold, what do you want to study?"

"Papa, I want to study the same lessons you give to others when you prepare them for baptism."

Trying not to act too excited, Siegfried asked, "When do you want to start?"

"Papa, if you're not too busy, I'd like to begin right now." *Praise the Lord.*

Harold brought his Bible and after praying together, father and son began to study. *I won't make any appointment for another study. I'll just wait and see what Harold does.*

The boy came back for another study the next day, the next, and the next. In a short time, they completed the entire set of lessons. *Now what am I going to do? My son's only nine, and I normally have children wait for baptism until they are 12 or 13!*

Stalling for more time, he suggested, "Harold, why don't we review the lessons to make sure you understand everything?"

"But Papa, you don't have other's do that," Harold blurted out in frustration.

"You see, Harold, following Jesus is the most important thing you can ever do. As your father, it's my responsibility to make sure you really understand what dedicating your life to Christ is all about."

After reviewing the first lesson, Harold went out to ride his bicycle. He raced downhill on the main street when the driver in a parked car suddenly opened the door. When Harold swerved to miss the door, his bike pedal ticked the edge of the car throwing him in the path of a speeding truck. Brakes screeched as the truck barely missed running over him.

An eight-inch gash on the boy's right leg bled profusely. The driver who opened the car door picked him up and drove him to his parent's house. Immediately his mother rushed him to the hospital where the doctor sutured the wound with 14 stitches. Siegfried wondered, *Will he give up studying the Bible now?*

Even in severe pain during the first few days, Harold kept going to his father for more Bible study. Healing in a tropical climate, with the possibility of infection, often proves a problem. To complicate matters, after the stitches were removed the gash partially opened up and needed to be cleaned out each day.

Weeks went by and the studies continued, but the wound didn't heal. Several times Harold asked, "Papa, may I be baptized now?"

Each time Siegfried replied, "No, not yet. You don't want to go into the river and risk getting infection. We've already had enough problems with your leg."

One Friday evening after sunset worship to welcome the Sabbath, Harold pulled up his pant leg. "Don't you think my leg's healed now?"

Siegfried and Evelyn looked carefully. "You're right, the skin is smooth; there's no more open sore. Your leg is completely healed."

Without hesitation, Harold turned to his dad. "Papa, may I be baptized tomorrow. I love Jesus and want Him to wash away all my sins."

"Tomorrow?" What could parents say? Siegfried and Evelyn had prayed daily for their son to choose to do God's will. "Let me check with members of the church board and share your request with them," Siegfried said.

Siegfried met with board members the next morning. One man said, "For a while, we thought your son might be having trouble with too much religion, but during the last few months we've noticed a great change and see him wanting to be faithful." They voted unanimously to recommend Harold's baptism.

That afternoon a happy father and son stood together in a jungle stream. Siegfried raised his hand. "My dear son, Harold. Because you love Jesus with all your heart and are determined to turn from the things of the world and with Christ's help obey God's commandments, I now baptize you in the name of the Father, Son, and Holy Spirit. Amen."

Tears flowed down Harold's cheeks as he walked out of the deep narrow stream. The boy stayed true to his vows. Today he serves as an occupational therapist at the Loma Linda Medical Center and is active in supporting the work of his church. He's dedicated to relieve human suffering and serve God in every possible way.

Two weeks after Harold's baptism, Siegfried announced a Communion service in his church at Quillabamba. Hearing this, Harold asked, "Papa, may I participate in the Communion service now? Will I be allowed to eat the bread and drink the grape juice?"

"Certainly, son," Siegfried responded. "You're a baptized member and understand the significance of feet washing and the Lord's Supper. I want you to always remember what the body and blood of Jesus mean to those who trust in Him."

Harold had another question. "Whose feet can I wash then?"

"Son, that depends on you. You choose the person you want to serve on this special occasion."

Harold looked at his dad. "May I wash your feet?" Father and son washing each other's feet established a permanent bond neither will forget. Siegfried realized that the Holy Spirit had worked on the heart of his active son all along.

⁓

While visiting his home church in Berlin, Siegfried kept thinking of his own baptism and what it meant to him: *I think that after dedicating my life to Christ here in Berlin, and being married to my wonderful wife, the greatest satisfaction in my life has been the privilege of baptizing my own son and daughter.*

The terrible war years left me with only three years of grade school. Later with God's help, I passed a GED test and completed four years of college in only three. It's amazing that with so little education, God allowed me to reach out to university students, professors, and many in the upper class during our years as missionaries in Peru.

Thinking about his life journey from burning Berlin and a lonely year at a Hitler Youth Camp to serving as an ordained minister, he marveled at God's leading. Perhaps one of the greatest joys in my ministry was to see primitive people in the Amazon totally change and prepare to live with Jesus in heaven.

Each time a student missionary spent time at the Unini Mission Station, he had determined to inspire them with the joys of seeing lives transformed. While attending a General Conference Session in Toronto, Siegfried heard Barry Black preach. *What a thrill to see*

*the young man from Oakwood College who traveled with me in a
dugout canoe, assisted with dental work, sang for evangelistic meetings, and helped me build a school. I can't believe he's Chief Chaplain
for the U. S. Navy.*

The two men embraced. "I thank God for what he has done in
your life!" Siegfried exclaimed.

Barry responded, "God put me with you and Evelyn; He put
me with two saints. I'll always be grateful for the influence of
your lives."

Today Barry Black is Chaplain of the U. S. Senate. God led
Barry's life in amazing ways allowing him, like Daniel, to stand
before government officials that might never have contact with a
true messenger of God in any other way.

Siegfried's own walk with Jesus began in Berlin largely through
the influence of a godly mother who stayed true to God all during
a difficult war. *What would I be doing now if Mutti hadn't taught
me to pray? Where would I be if she hadn't risked her life to get me
out of the Hitler Youth Camp before the Russians took over? God
inspired my mother to get me on the last train out of Poland before
the war ended. No one has ever heard of the other boys who were
there with me.*

Still visiting in Berlin, Siegfried and Evelyn drove to his birthplace. Streets in the booming city changed so much since his
childhood that he had difficulty finding the place. When they
finally reached the site, Siegfried looked in astonishment. "The
house is gone!" The place where he took his first breath, the
home where his family survived bursting bombs during a terrible
war … gone!

Siegfried squeezed Evelyn's hand. "What a disappointment! I
wanted to see it one more time." Instead of the old wood frame
home built by his father, they looked at a modern apartment building. Apartment house! They'd almost forgotten. Back in Loma
Linda, there's an empty lot.

Before going as volunteer missionaries to Peru, they purchased a lot next to their home, planning to build an apartment
complex with nine apartments. This would give them guaranteed
income and financial security for the rest of their lives. God had
other plans. The empty lot remains, but the nine apartments they
dreamed about will never be built. They don't have the money, and

if they did, new zoning restrictions will not permit the construction they planned.

Instead of owning their own apartment complex, they dedicated their lives to help people get ready to live in the Celestial Townhouses Jesus is preparing for all who love Him. The Savior says, "In My Father's house are many mansions. ... I go to prepare a place for you. And if I go and prepare a place for you, I will come again and receive you to Myself; that where I am, *there* you may be also" (John 14:1–3).

It gets better. After Jesus re-creates our planet, those who live in the Holy City's mansions will be able to build their own dream homes. "They shall build houses and inhabit *them*. ... My elect shall long enjoy the work of their hands" (Isaiah 65:21, 22).

"God's Word is true," Siegfried said. "Seek first the kingdom of God and His righteousness, and all these things shall be added to you. To be with Jesus is worth a lot more than anything this world offers."

Leaving the site of his childhood home and memories of the horrors of war, they drove away watching the apartments disappear, just like their plan to build apartments on the empty lot in Loma Linda had vanished.

Evelyn smiled, "We made the right choice."

Siegfried held his wife. "And thank you for being part of that choice. My prayer will always be, 'Make me a blessing to someone.'"